Don't Buy Their Lunch, Buy Their Loyalty

The Daily Habits That Actually Retain Employees

By Sharon Grossman, PhD

Warrior Publishing, LLC

ISBN: 978-1-952437-06-9

Contents

Preface: The $365 Problem

≈

I was sitting in the back of a hotel ballroom watching a consultant deliver a full-day leadership retreat. Breakfast was continental. Lunch was catered. The PowerPoint deck had 127 slides.

By 2:00 PM, half the room was checking email. By 3:30 PM, the facilitator was competing with side conversations. By 4:45 PM, people were already packing up laptops fifteen minutes early.

Three months later, I asked the VP who sponsored it what changed.

"Honestly? Nothing. We got some good ideas, but everyone went back to their desks and fell into the same routines."

Thousand of dollars. Eight hours. Eighty-five leaders. Zero behavioral change.

This is the $365 problem.

The Illusion of the Big Investment

Most organizations approach culture and leadership development the same way people approach New Year's resolutions. They make one big commitment, usually in January, convince themselves this is the year everything changes, and then wonder why by March everyone has forgotten what was even discussed.

The annual leadership retreat. The once-a-year training. The holiday party where the CEO gives the "we're all family" speech. The consultant who flies in, drops some frameworks, and flies out.

We treat culture like it's something you can install during a maintenance window.

Here's what actually happens: You spend thousands on a retreat. Leaders feel inspired for about a week. They go back to putting out fires. The binder from the training sits on a shelf. By quarter two, nobody remembers the theme. By quarter four, you're planning next year's event, hoping this time it'll stick.

You just spent $365 once instead of $1 every day.

The Compound Effect Nobody Talks About

Let me show you something.

If you invest $365 once at the beginning of the year in a savings account earning 5% interest, by year-end you'll have $383.13.

If you invest $1 every single day for 365 days in that same account, you'll have $387.49.

Not a huge difference on the surface, at least in dollars and cents. But when it comes to your people, the gap is much wider.

By investing in your team just once a year, here's what happens:

Every day you don't reinforce what matters, you're not just staying flat. You're losing ground. Skills decay. Priorities shift. Bad habits creep back in. The culture defaults to whatever's easiest, not what's best.

One big training session per year compounds at maybe 2% if you're lucky, because there's no repetition, no reinforcement, no daily practice.

A small, consistent daily practice compounds at 20%, 30%, sometimes 50% because it builds muscle memory. It creates systems. It makes the right behaviors automatic.

What This Book Is Not

This isn't another book about "culture" that tells you to paint motivational quotes on the walls and have more pizza parties.

This isn't a book about engagement surveys that produce 47-page reports nobody reads.

This isn't a book about complicated change management frameworks that require a doctorate to implement.

This is a book about five simple habits that take ten to fifteen minutes a day and produce measurable results in weeks, not years.

I know that sounds too good to be true. Stick with me.

What Changed My Mind

I used to believe in big events, too. I've delivered plenty of them. Good content. Engaged audiences. Solid evaluations.

And then I started tracking what actually changed six months later. The honest answer was: not much.

So I started experimenting with something different. What if instead of giving leaders a one-day workshop, I gave them a fifteen-minute daily structure? What if instead of an annual engagement survey, we checked in every single day? What if instead of a quarterly recognition program, we built appreciation into the daily routine?

The results were uncomfortably clear.

A hospital reduced turnover from 49% to 8% in 36 months. Similarly, a fast food company cut turnover from 300% to 45% in 18 months. They didn't change pay. They didn't change benefits. They changed what leaders did for fifteen minutes every morning.

Airports using the same methodology saw employee satisfaction go up by up to 31% and customer satisfaction increase by up to 33% in just 2-3 months.

The secret? Five habits that happened every single shift.

These weren't companies with unlimited budgets or fancy headquarters. They were organizations that stopped making annual bets and started making daily deposits.

The Five Habits That Compound

This book is built around five habits. Easy to remember: Together they spell HABIT:

- **H** - Huddles
- **A** - Appreciation
- **B** - Barometer
- **I** - Improvement Opportunities
- **T** - Tracking

Each one takes minutes. Combined, they create a system that compounds daily.

And here's what makes this different from every other leadership book you've read: this system is measurable. You can track it with a simple spreadsheet, or you can use the Habit app we developed specifically for this methodology—a tool that makes tracking effortless and gives you real-time insights into what's actually happening with your team.

The app shows you instantly when someone's mood drops before it becomes a resignation. It tracks who's being recognized and who's being overlooked. It monitors which problems are getting fixed and which are being ignored. It turns invisible culture work into visible data that predicts outcomes.

You don't need the app to make this work. But it makes the difference between hoping you're building culture and knowing you are.

You just need ten to fifteen minutes tomorrow morning and the discipline to do it again the next day.

Who This Book Is For

If you're a frontline leader (supervisor, manager, team lead), this book will give you a system that makes your job easier, not harder. You'll know exactly what to do each day to build your team without adding more meetings or paperwork.

If you're an executive, this book will show you how to drive culture change without waiting for HR to roll out another initiative. You'll get leading indicators that actually predict problems before they show up in your quarterly numbers.

If you're in HR or Operations, this book gives you a framework that works across industries and doesn't require you to convince people to care about "engagement." You'll be measuring things that executives actually pay attention to: turnover, safety, quality, efficiency.

If you've already read Jorge Torres's book on the Performance Habit (the methodology this approach is built on), consider this the practical implementation guide focused specifically on the daily habits that make it work. If you haven't, get a copy.

A Promise and a Challenge

I'm going to make you a promise: If you implement these five habits consistently for ninety days, you will see measurable improvement in at least two of these areas: turnover, quality, safety, efficiency, or employee satisfaction.

Not "people will feel better." Not "culture will improve." Actual numbers will move.

But here's the challenge: You have to do it every day. You can't skip the daily deposit and expect compound returns.

Most leadership books end up on shelves because they're too complicated to implement or too vague to measure. This one is neither.

You'll learn by Chapter 4 exactly what to do Monday morning. You'll learn in Chapter 8 how to measure if it's working. You'll know by the end of the book whether this is worth the investment.

The question isn't whether this works. I've got the data.

The question is whether you're willing to make the daily deposit.

Let's find out.

Note: Throughout this book, I'll share real examples from real companies. Names and identifying details have been changed to protect the guilty and the innocent alike. The numbers are real. The lessons are universal.

PART 1

The Case For Daily Deposits

CHAPTER 1

Why Willpower Fails and Habits Win

～～

You don't decide to check your phone when it buzzes. You just do it. You don't consciously choose your route to work every morning. Your hands turn the wheel automatically. You don't think about how to tie your shoes. Your fingers know the pattern.

This isn't laziness. It's efficiency.

In 2006, Duke University researcher Wendy Wood published a study that revealed something remarkable: more than 40% of the actions you perform each day aren't actual decisions. They're habits. Your brain has automated them to conserve mental energy.

Think about that for a moment. Nearly half of what you do every day is running on autopilot.

This is why leadership development fails so spectacularly. We treat behavior change like a decision problem—give people better information, stronger motivation, clearer frameworks—and assume they'll choose to act differently.

But that's not how humans work.

Your managers aren't failing because they lack willpower. They're failing because you're asking them to override habits with decisions. And decisions lose to habits every single time.

The Habit Loop That Runs Your Organization

Habits follow a simple pattern: cue, routine, reward.

You see a cue (your phone buzzes), you follow a routine (check the message), you get a reward (information or social connection). Do this enough times, and your brain automates it. The cue triggers the routine without conscious thought.

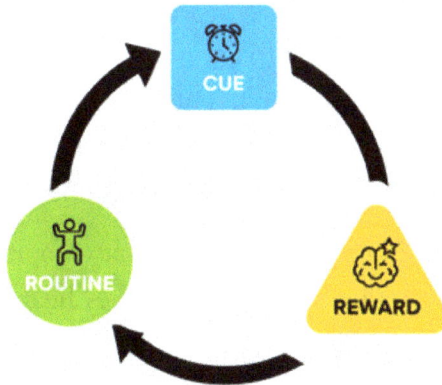

Leadership behaviors work exactly the same way.

The way a supervisor starts their shift. How they respond when an employee raises a problem. Whether they acknowledge good work or only point out mistakes. When they choose to communicate priorities.

These aren't thoughtful decisions made fresh each day. They're habits. Built through repetition in a specific environment, triggered by specific cues, reinforced by specific rewards.

And here's the critical insight most organizations miss: you can't change habits by teaching people to make better decisions. You have to change the architecture that creates the habits in the first place.

What the Forgetting Curve Reveals

In 1885, German psychologist Hermann Ebbinghaus discovered something that should have changed how we think about training forever: humans forget approximately 70% of new information within 24 hours unless it's actively reinforced. [2][3][4]

Our brains are constantly triaging information, keeping what's useful and discarding what isn't. The criteria for "useful" is simple: repetition and application. If you don't use information repeatedly in a relevant context, your brain assumes it doesn't matter.

Research on learning retention shows that people remember only 10% of what they read and 20% of what they hear in a presentation. Retention jumps to 75% when people practice the skill themselves, and 90% when they teach it to others. [1][6]

Conferences, annual retreats, leadership bootcamps often provide great content. People take notes. They have insights. But when they return to their desks, there's no system to reinforce those insights. No daily practice. No environmental cues triggering the new behaviors. No rewards for executing the frameworks.

Within a week, 90% of what they learned is gone. [2]

Not because your people aren't motivated. Because that's what brains do.

The Real Math

Let's examine what a big once-a-year event actually buys.

The company gets two days of focused attention from—let's say—120 managers. If 10% of them implemented even one new practice for a month (an optimistic estimate), that's 12 managers trying something different. Most will revert to old habits within weeks.

THE LEARNING PYRAMID
How people retain information

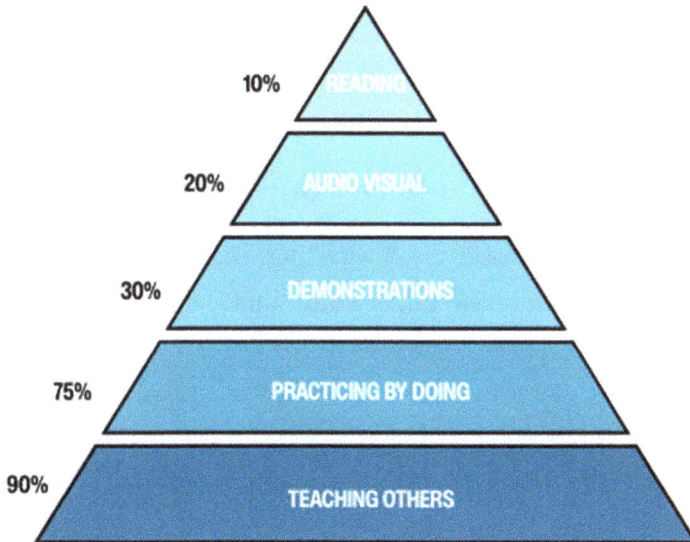

10% READING

20% AUDIO VISUAL

30% DEMONSTRATIONS

75% PRACTICING BY DOING

90% TEACHING OTHERS

Now consider an alternative: What if each manager spent 15 minutes daily practicing specific leadership behaviors—recognizing employees, aligning priorities, catching problems early?

ANNUAL TRAINING MODEL:

120 leaders × 2 days = 240 leadership development days per year

DAILY PRACTICE MODEL:

120 leaders × 15 minutes × 250 work days = 7,500 hours annually

But the real difference isn't time. It's repetition.

The annual model gives you one exposure to new concepts. The daily model gives you 250 repetitions—enough for those behaviors to become automatic habits anchored in the actual work environment.

This is the compound effect of habit formation. Small actions repeated consistently create exponential results. Large actions taken sporadically create nothing.

What Companies Are Really Buying

If annual training events rarely produce behavior change, why do companies keep spending billions on them? [5]

The answer reveals something fascinating about organizational decision-making.

Companies aren't buying behavior change. They're buying four things:

1. **Visible action.** Events are tangible. You can see them happening. There are photos, hashtags, attendance records. Daily practice is invisible. It doesn't generate newsletter content or impress the board.

2. **Simplified decision-making.** Writing one check for an annual event is easier than building a system that changes

what 120 leaders do every single day. One decision versus sustained infrastructure.

3. **Psychological comfort.** When turnover spikes, executives can point to the training budget and say, "We invested in our people." It's organizational cover. Proof that leadership cares, even if metrics don't improve.

4. **Hope over evidence.** The belief that *this* speaker, *this* framework, *this* retreat will finally be different. Hope is cheaper than admitting that the entire model doesn't work.

This creates a cycle: Event → No change → Different event → No change → Repeat.

Organizations are trapped in what behavioral economists call "action bias"—the tendency to favor action over inaction even when the action is ineffective. Doing something feels better than doing nothing, even when that something predictably fails.

The Alternative Architecture

The solution isn't better training events. It's a different architecture for behavior change.

Consider how you learned to drive. You didn't attend an intensive weekend seminar and emerge a skilled driver. You practiced consistently in the environment where driving happens—on actual roads—with immediate feedback, until the behaviors became automatic.

Leadership development works the same way. Sustainable behavior change requires:

1. **Specific behaviors practiced in context.** Not frameworks discussed in hotels, but actions performed on the distribution center floor.

2. **Daily repetition.** Enough frequency for the behavior to become habitual, not aspirational.

3. **Environmental cues.** Triggers that prompt the new routine in the moment it's needed.

4. **Immediate rewards.** Feedback that reinforces the behavior, making it more likely to repeat.

This is why a 15-minute daily practice beats a two-day annual event. Not because 15 minutes contains more information, but because 250 repetitions build habits while two days build binders.

The math is stark: over five years, the annual model produces roughly 60 attempted behavior changes. The daily model produces 150,000 repetitions.

That's a fundamentally different approach to how behavior change happens.

The Uncomfortable Truth

Most corporate training is designed to make executives feel like they're addressing problems, not to actually change behavior.

If organizations genuinely believed behavior change required daily practice and environmental reinforcement, they wouldn't keep investing in annual events that violate everything we know about habit formation.

The event satisfies the organizational need to "do something" while requiring minimal ongoing commitment. It's expensive theater that creates the appearance of progress without the architecture for change.

But here's what's interesting: once you understand the habit loop—cue, routine, reward—you can redesign how leadership development actually works.

Instead of teaching frameworks in isolation, you can build specific behaviors into the daily routine. Instead of hoping managers remember what they learned, you can create environmental cues that trigger the desired behaviors. Instead of measuring satisfaction with training, you can track whether the behaviors are actually happening.

This requires more discipline but less budget. More consistency but less drama. More daily deposits but fewer grand gestures.

It's not that annual events have no value. Strategic alignment matters. Face-to-face connection matters. But if you're doing the event *instead of* daily practice, you're choosing comfort over effectiveness.

Where Change Actually Lives

You can start tomorrow. You don't need a huge budget. You don't need a hotel ballroom. You don't need to fly anyone anywhere.

You need fifteen minutes, a specific behavior to practice, and the discipline to show up the next day.

That's where change lives.

The question isn't whether you're investing in leadership development. The question is whether that investment is building habits or just building hope.

▶ Red Flag:

If your organization measures training effectiveness through satisfaction surveys instead of behavior change metrics, you're optimizing for the wrong outcome. Happy attendees don't equal changed habits.

Reflection Questions

1. What leadership behaviors do you want to change, and how are you currently reinforcing them daily?

2. Can you name three specific habits your best leaders practice consistently that your struggling leaders don't?

3. If you tracked leadership behaviors daily for 90 days, what would the data reveal about consistency?

Chapter 1 References:

[1] BizLibrary. "Learning Retention: The Key to Employee Training." https://www.bizlibrary.com/blog/learning-methods/learning-retention-key-employee-training/

[2] Knowledge Anywhere. "Seventy Percent of Your Training is Forgotten: Learn the Science of Knowledge Retention." https://knowledgeanywhere.com/articles/seventy-percent-of-your-training-is-forgotten-learn-the-science-of-knowledge-retention-and-how-it-affects-online-training/

[3] WayWeDo. "The Forgetting Curve: Why Documentation and Training Fails." https://www.waywedo.com/blog/forgetting-curve/

[4] Tallyfy. "Why Documentation Training Fails: The Forgetting Curve." https://tallyfy.com/products/pro/tutorials/why-documentation-training-fails-forgetting-curve/

[5] eLearning Industry. "Employee Training Statistics, Trends and Data." https://elearningindustry.com/employee-training-statistics-trends-and-data

[6] Ferris State University. "How to Retain 90% of Everything You Learn." https://www.ferris.edu/university-college/firstgen/student-handbook/howtoretain90.pdf

What Gets Measured Gets Managed

(What Gets Repeated Gets Results)

⚬≈≈⚬

The VP of Operations was staring at his quarterly dashboard like it had personally insulted him.

"Turnover is at 82%. Safety incidents are up 14%. Quality defects increased 9%. Employee satisfaction dropped six points."

He looked up at me. "We're doing worse than last quarter. What do we need to fix?"

"Wrong question," I said.

"What's the right question?" He had this confused look in his eyes.

"What are your leaders doing every day?"

He blinked. "What do you mean?"

"I mean, what specific behaviors are your frontline supervisors repeating daily that would drive those numbers?"

Long pause.

"I don't know."

And that's the problem.

The Lagging Indicator Trap

Every organization measures outcomes:

- Turnover rate
- Safety incidents
- Quality scores
- Customer satisfaction
- Revenue
- Profit margin

These are called lagging indicators because they tell you what already happened. They're the scoreboard. They're useful for knowing if you're winning or losing, but they're useless for telling you what to do differently tomorrow morning.

It's like trying to lose weight by only stepping on the scale. The number tells you the result, but it doesn't tell you whether to eat less, move more, sleep better, or manage stress. You're measuring the output without controlling the inputs.

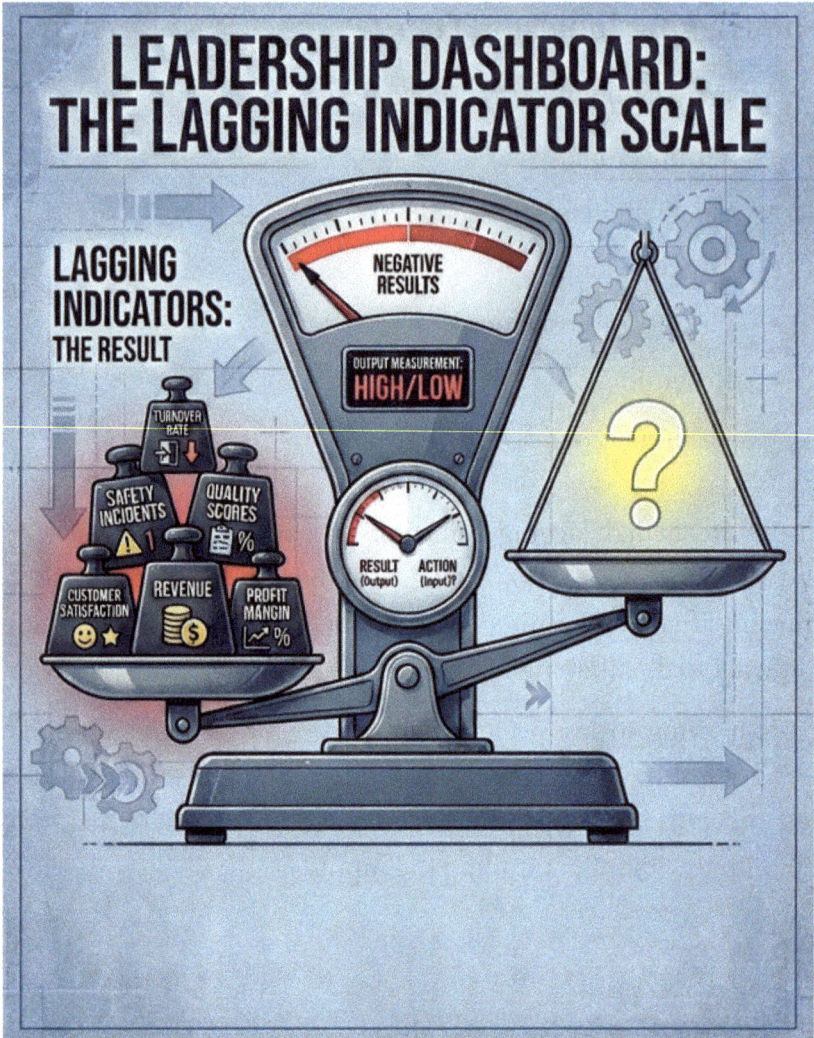

Most leadership dashboards are nothing but lagging indicators. By the time you see the problem in the data, it's already cost you money, people, or both.

Here's what that VP didn't know: his turnover rate wasn't the problem. It was the symptom.

The problem was that his frontline supervisors weren't doing anything specific, measurable, or consistent to make employees want to stay. They were reacting to fires, managing logistics, and hoping engagement would somehow take care of itself.

Hope is not a retention strategy.

Inputs vs. Outputs: The Only Equation That Matters

If you want to change outputs, you have to change inputs.

Outputs are what you get. Inputs are what you do.

Want lower turnover? You need to change what leaders do every day that affects whether people stay or leave.

Want better safety numbers? You need to change the daily behaviors that prevent incidents.

Want higher quality? You need to change the coaching and process reinforcement that happens on the floor.

But here's where most organizations fail: they measure outputs religiously and inputs barely at all.

They track turnover monthly but couldn't tell you how many employees got recognized this week.

They measure safety incidents but don't track how many safety conversations supervisors had.

They're driving by looking in the rearview mirror and wondering why they keep hitting things.

The Three Employee Motivators

So what are the inputs that actually matter?

After studying organizational behavior across industries, researchers have consistently identified three core psychological needs that drive employee engagement, retention, and performance. Together, they spell BAR, and the goal is simple: we need to raise the BAR.

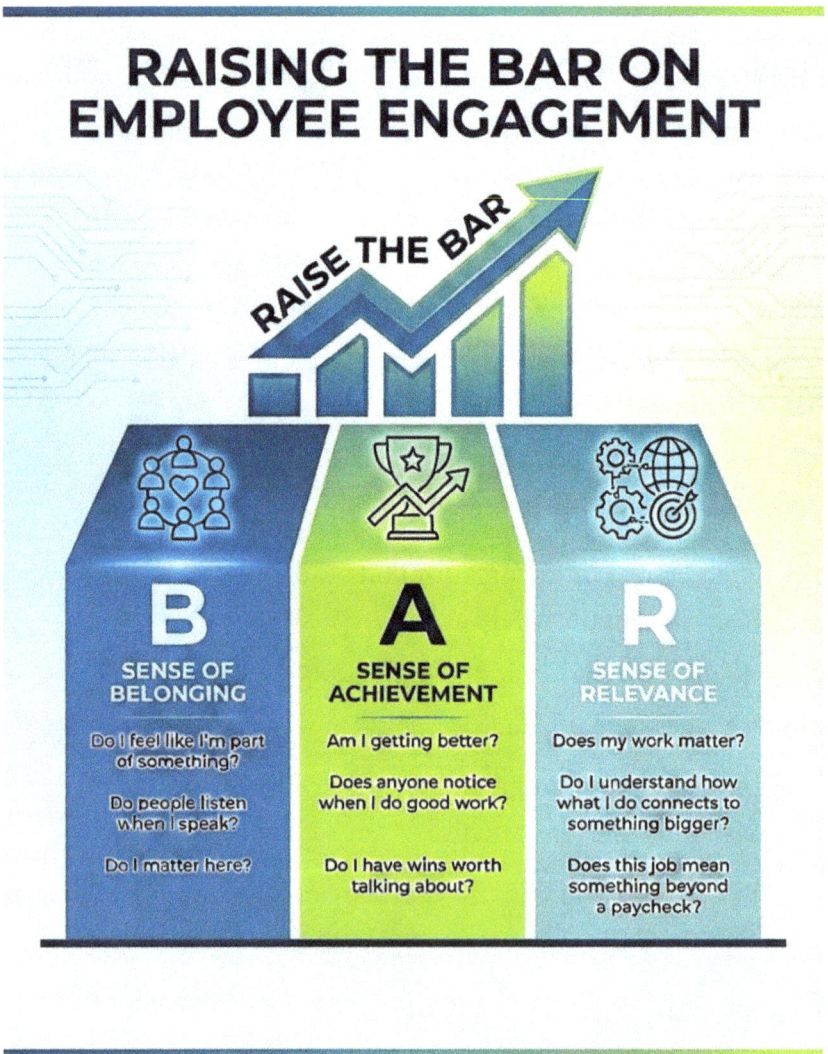

RAISING THE BAR ON EMPLOYEE ENGAGEMENT

RAISE THE BAR

B
SENSE OF BELONGING

Do I feel like I'm part of something?

Do people listen when I speak?

Do I matter here?

A
SENSE OF ACHIEVEMENT

Am I getting better?

Does anyone notice when I do good work?

Do I have wins worth talking about?

R
SENSE OF RELEVANCE

Does my work matter?

Do I understand how what I do connects to something bigger?

Does this job mean something beyond a paycheck?

1. SENSE OF BELONGING

Do I feel like I'm part of something? Do people listen when I speak? Do I matter here?

2. SENSE OF ACHIEVEMENT

Am I getting better? Does anyone notice when I do good work? Do I have wins worth talking about?

3. SENSE OF RELEVANCE

Does my work matter? Do I understand how what I do connects to something bigger? Does this job mean something beyond a paycheck?

These are hardwired human needs that directly predict whether someone will stay at your company or leave.

Study after study confirms this. People don't leave jobs because of pay alone. They leave because they feel invisible, irrelevant, or stagnant. They leave because nobody noticed when they showed up, nobody cared what they contributed, and nobody recognized when they improved.

The data is clear: employees who feel a strong sense of belonging are 50% less likely to leave. Employees who receive regular recognition have 31% lower voluntary turnover. Employees who understand the purpose of their work show 30% higher engagement scores.[7][8]

Now here's the uncomfortable truth: most organizations do nothing systematic to create belonging, achievement, or relevance. They mention it in the employee handbook. They talk about it at town halls. But they don't measure whether it's actually happening on the frontline every single day.

They're hoping their supervisors naturally create these experiences. Some do. Most don't. And nobody knows the difference until people quit.

When you systematically raise the BAR (Belonging, Achievement, Relevance) every day, retention follows. When you don't, turnover becomes your most expensive lagging indicator.

Why Frontline Leaders Are Your Highest-Leverage Investment

You know who has more influence over whether an employee stays or leaves than anyone else in the company?

Not the CEO. Not HR. Not total compensation.

Their direct supervisor.

Research from Gallup shows that managers account for 70% of the variance in employee engagement.[9] If you have a great supervisor, you'll tolerate mediocre pay, outdated equipment, and bureaucratic nonsense. If you have a terrible supervisor, no amount of free lunches will make you stay.

Your frontline leaders are the delivery system for belonging, achievement, and relevance. They're the ones who make employees feel seen, valued, and capable. Or they don't. They're the ones responsible for raising the BAR every single day.

The problem is that most organizations promote people to supervisor because they were good at the job, not because they know how to lead. Then they give them zero structure, minimal training, and no accountability for actually developing their people.

We expect them to figure it out. But in reality, they are busy managing logistics and putting out fires, which means the "people stuff" gets deprioritized.

This is insane when you think about it.

You're losing 80% of your workforce every year in some industries. The cost to replace an hourly employee ranges from $3,500 to $7,500 depending on the role. For a distribution center with 200 employees at 80% turnover, that's $1.12 million in replacement costs annually.

And the solution is sitting right there: teach your frontline leaders five simple habits they can execute in fifteen minutes a day that systematically create belonging, achievement, and relevance. Raise the BAR consistently, and retention follows.

If you cut turnover from 80% to 40%, you just saved $560,000 per year. Per location.

That's math.

What Gets Repeated Gets Results

Here's the equation that changes everything:

Consistent daily inputs → predictable outputs

If you want different results, change what gets repeated.

Most organizations try to change results directly. They set goals. They create initiatives. They measure outcomes harder. It doesn't work because they're not changing the daily behaviors that produce those outcomes.

The Performance Habit flips this through daily behaviors that create belonging, achievement, and relevance. It makes those behaviors easy, structured, and measurable. It holds leaders accountable for doing them consistently. It raises the BAR systematically instead of hoping it happens accidentally.

Input metrics are leading indicators. They tell you what's about to happen before it shows up in the lagging indicators. They give you time to intervene. They put you in control.

Tracking What Matters

You can track these five daily habits with a spreadsheet. Some organizations do. But we built something better.

The Habit app turns leading indicators into real-time visibility. Here's what it does:

When employees scan the QR code at the start of the huddle, leaders see the team's mood instantly.

It automatically generates a top 10 list of the most recognized employees. You know exactly who's getting seen and who's getting ignored.

It tracks improvement opportunities: how many were brought up, how many got completed, how many are still outstanding. No more sticky notes or good intentions that disappear.

When customers scan a QR code, their satisfaction data flows into a color-coded bar graph with their comments. You can see patterns before they become problems.

The app makes those daily habits visible. It turns behavior into data. It gives you early warning signals instead of quarterly autopsies.

You don't need the app to make this work. But it helps you see what's working before the lagging indicators tell you what already failed.

The Turning Point

When that VP finally understood this, he asked, "So what should I be measuring?"

"Five things," I said.

1. Are your leaders doing daily huddles?
2. Are they recognizing people?
3. Are they checking the team mood?
4. Are they capturing and resolving improvement opportunities?
5. Are they tracking the data?"

"That's it?"

"That's it. Because if they do those five things consistently, your lagging indicators will fix themselves."

He tried it. Six months later, his dashboard looked completely different.

Turns out Peter Drucker was right: what gets measured gets managed.

And what gets repeated gets results.

And if you want results that compound, you need to repeat the right things every single day.

⚡ Quick Win:

Pick one lagging indicator you're trying to improve (turnover, safety, quality, engagement). Now identify one daily behavior that, if done consistently by frontline leaders, would directly influence that metric. That's your first input to measure.

🚩 Red Flag:

If your leadership dashboard only shows lagging indicators (results from last week, last month, last quarter), you're driving blind. You have no early warning system and no ability to course-correct before problems become expensive.

Reflection Questions

1. What percentage of your leadership dashboard is lagging indicators vs. leading indicators?

2. Can you name three specific daily behaviors your frontline supervisors are doing that create belonging, relevance, or achievement?

3. If you asked your employees whether they feel seen, valued, and capable, what percentage would say yes?

4. How much money are you spending annually to replace employees who leave? What would you save if you cut that number in half?

5. What would change if you measured what your leaders do every day instead of only measuring business outcomes?

Chapter 2 References:

[7] BetterUp. "The Value of Belonging at Work: Investing in Workplace Inclusion." https://www.betterup.com/blog/the-value-of-belonging-at-work

[8] Gallup. "How to Improve Employee Engagement in the Workplace." https://www.gallup.com/workplace/285674/improve-employee-engagement-workplace.aspx

[9] Gallup. "State of the American Manager: Analytics and Advice for Leaders." https://www.gallup.com/workplace/231593/state-american-manager-report.aspx

CHAPTER 3
The Performance Habit Framework

෴

A plant manager once asked me, "How many things do my supervisors need to do differently?"

"Five," I said.

"That's it?"

"That's it."

"What if we added a few more? We've got some other initiatives we're trying to — "

"No," I interrupted. "Five. Not seven. Not twelve. Five."

He looked skeptical. "Seems too simple."

"Simple is the point. Complex doesn't scale. Complex doesn't stick. Complex gets abandoned the moment someone gets busy."

Eighteen months later, after cutting turnover in half, he told me, "I'm glad you didn't let me complicate it."

The Five HABIT Components

THE PERFORMANCE HABIT FRAMEWORK
Five Daily Behaviors for Frontline Leaders | Approx. 10-15 Minutes Per Day

H - Huddles
Creates Relevance
- A structured daily meeting at the start of each shift.
- Short, intentional, and a systematic way to reinforce purpose, preview the day, and connect work to meaning.

A - Appreciation
Creates Achievement

Daily recognition of specific, observable behaviors. Immediate, specific acknowledgment of what people did right today.

B - Barometer
Creates Belonging

A daily mood check where employees scan a QR code to indicate how they're feeling: good, okay, or struggling. Leaders get real-time data on morale to intervene early.

I - Improvement Opportunities
Reinforces Belonging

A daily question: "What's preventing you from doing an even better job?" Employees identify obstacles. Leaders log them. Things get fixed. Employees see their voice matters.

T - Tracking
Creates Accountability and Visibility

Logging the data from your huddle into the system. who attended, recognitions given, barometer results, improvement opportunities raised. Leaders can't fake it. Executives see frontline reality in real-time.

The Performance Habit framework consists of five daily behaviors that frontline leaders implement in approximately 10-15 minutes per day. Together, they spell HABIT:

H - HUDDLES

A structured daily meeting at the start of each shift. This is different from a typical meeting. It's short, intentional, and a systematic way to reinforce the behaviors you want your team to engage in, connect work to purpose, and preview the day. This creates Relevance.

A - APPRECIATION

Daily recognition of specific, observable behaviors. This includes immediate, specific acknowledgment of what people did right today. This creates Achievement.

B - BAROMETER

A daily mood check where employees scan a QR code to indicate how they're feeling: good, okay, or struggling. Leaders get real-time data on morale and can intervene before small problems become resignation letters. This creates Belonging.

I - IMPROVEMENT OPPORTUNITIES

A daily question: "What's preventing you from doing an even better job?" Employees identify obstacles. Leaders log them. Things get fixed. Employees see that their voice matters. This reinforces Relevance and Belonging.

T - TRACKING

Logging the data from your huddle into the system: who attended, what recognitions were given, barometer results, what improvement opportunities were raised. This creates accountability and visibility. Leaders can't fake it. Executives can see what's actually happening on the frontline in real-time.

Five components. Each one takes minutes. Together, they systematically raise the BAR every single day.

Why HABIT Works When Everything Else Fails

Most culture initiatives fail for three reasons:

1. THEY'RE TOO COMPLICATED.

Nobody can remember what they're supposed to do, so nothing happens consistently.

2. THEY'RE TOO INFREQUENT.

Annual events don't change behavior. Monthly check-ins don't create habits. Daily repetition does.

3. THEY'RE NOT MEASURABLE.

"Improve engagement" isn't a behavior. "Do a daily huddle" is. You can track it. You can coach it. You can hold people accountable for it.

The Performance Habit framework solves all three problems.

It's simple enough to remember without notes. Five components. Five letters. HABIT.

It's daily, so it compounds through repetition instead of evaporating between events.

It's completely measurable and trackable.

- Did the leader do the huddle today? Yes or no.
- Did they log it? Yes or no.
- Did they recognize anyone? Yes or no.
- Did they check the barometer? Yes or no.

You can track compliance. And because it's simple, daily, and measurable, it actually gets done.

The Framework Is the Foundation

The next five chapters will break down each component in detail. You'll learn exactly how to run a huddle, how to give meaningful recognition, how to use the barometer, how to track improvement opportunities, and how to log everything so you have data, not just good intentions.

But before we dive into the mechanics, understand this: the framework works because it's designed for humans, not spreadsheets.

⚡ Quick Win:

Monday morning, write down the names of your direct reports. Next to each name, write one specific thing they did well this week. Tomorrow morning, gather your team for five minutes, recognize those behaviors publicly, and log who you recognized in a simple spreadsheet or notebook. Congratulations, you just did your first huddle with appreciation and tracking. Do it again Tuesday.

🚩 Red Flag:

If you find yourself thinking, "This is too simple to make a difference," you're confusing simple with easy. Simple means executable. Easy means effortless. The framework is simple. Doing it daily for 90 days isn't easy. But it works.

Reflection Questions

1. What's preventing you from starting a daily huddle on Monday morning?

2. How many culture initiatives has your organization started in the past three years? How many are still running consistently?

3. If you started logging your daily leadership activities today, what would the data reveal about your consistency?

PART 2

The 5 Habit System

CHAPTER 4

H - Huddles

(Daily Dialogues)

⁓

Richard Branson walks into a conference room and removes all the chairs. His leadership team looks confused. "Where are we supposed to sit?"

"You're not," Branson says. "Standing meetings only. If everyone's standing, we stay focused and brief."

Virgin Group has been running standing meetings for years. Facebook does 15-minute daily stand-ups. Marissa Mayer instituted 5-10 minute "micro-meetings" at Yahoo to force concise decision-making.

These companies figured out something important: when you change the format, you change the effectiveness.

At Turnkey Retention Solutions, we call them Huddles or Daily Dialogues rather than a meeting.

A meeting is transactional. A dialogue is relational. A meeting broadcasts information. A dialogue creates connection. And most importantly, a dialogue happens every single day.

The Daily Dialogue is the foundation of the Performance Habit system. It's where culture gets built fifteen minutes at a time.

But it doesn't start at 7 a.m. on the production floor. It starts weeks earlier, in a conference room with a frontline supervisor who's probably been promoted three months ago because they were good at their job, not because they were good at leading people.

The Accidental Leader Problem

Here's what typically happens when someone gets promoted to frontline supervisor:

Day 1: Congratulations, you're a leader now. Here's your team.

Day 2: Go lead them.

Day 30: Why isn't anyone engaged?

Most new supervisors start leading with the same amount of preparation you'd get before operating a waffle iron. Roughly 60–82% step into the role with zero formal training. [10] One major study even labeled two-thirds of managers "accidental"…which explains why one in three employees eventually bail. [11] And when training does exist, it's often a few hours a month. Basically the leadership equivalent of a snack, not a meal.

So we get accidental leaders. Good people. Wrong tools.

And they default to one of two styles:

The Taskmaster: "Do the work. Questions? No? Great."

The Buddy: "Hey everyone. So. Stuff. Yeah?"

Neither one builds culture. Neither one creates daily deposits. Neither one taps into what really drives performance: Belonging, Relevance, Achievement.

The Daily Dialogue fixes this. It gives the accidental leader a framework so simple it's basically leadership-by-numbers.

The Board: Your Leadership Cheat Sheet

Before the first huddle, we create a board customized for your team. It lives on the wall, like a North Star, but without the astronomy degree.

The board does three things:

- It tells the leader how to structure the huddle.

- It keeps them on track so they don't start talking about their cat.

- It ensures the experience is consistent no matter who's leading.

It's leadership with bumpers on the bowling lane.

Training Before the First Meeting

The Daily Dialogue doesn't work if you just hand someone a board and say "good luck." It requires a focused, pragmatic training process that happens before the first meeting ever takes place.

Step 1: The "Why" Presentation: Leaders are exposed to a reduced version of the methodology that explains why they're doing this. Not the full academic dissertation, just enough context to understand the three motivators (Belonging, Relevance, Achievement) and why daily repetition beats annual training every single time.

Step 2: Board Familiarization: The trainer walks the leader through the customized Daily Dialogue board, section by section. They explain what each section does, why it's there, and how it connects to the methodology.

Then comes the critical part: process flow. The trainer shows the leader exactly where to start, where to move next, and where to finish.

The board is typically organized around three key sections: People, Operation, and Performance. Within these sections, leaders will discuss the organization's Purpose and Values, share Company News from senior leadership, address operational information relevant to that day's work, and review Key Performance Indicators.

The board also includes a calendar or rotation of specific, observable behaviors tied to the organization's values. These are concrete, visible actions that demonstrate what your values actually look like in practice. Instead of a vague value like "Respect," the board might show behaviors like "I make eye contact when someone is speaking to me" or "I clean up after myself in shared spaces."

Every day, the leader prompts a brief dialogue about one or two of these behaviors. They might ask, "What does that behavior mean to you?" The behaviors rotate on a calendar, cycling through 15 to 30 different behaviors over the course of a month. This creates the repetition necessary for behavioral hardwiring: human brains require five to seven exposures before something becomes automatic.

The leader doesn't need to invent the structure or come up with behaviors on their own. They just need to follow what's already built into the board.

Step 3: Behavioral Modeling: Leaders watch videos of other leaders conducting the Daily Dialogue. Even if the video is from a different industry (a hospital example when you're in construction, a manufacturing example when you're in hospitality), the fundamentals translate.

They're coached on specific execution details:

- Face the people, not the board
- Ask open-ended questions to generate dialogue
- Keep it tight: 15 minutes, maximum

This is where leaders learn the difference between presenting information and facilitating a conversation.

WHAT THE TRAINING ACHIEVES

Three things:

Objective 1: Behavioral Hardwiring

The goal isn't to teach. It's to preach. The Daily Dialogue succeeds through repetition. This training prepares leaders to be the mechanism of repetition.

Objective 2: Communication Infrastructure

The Daily Dialogue creates a two-way communication channel. Downstream: senior leadership's messages reach 100% of frontline employees. Upstream: frontline feedback reaches decision-makers.

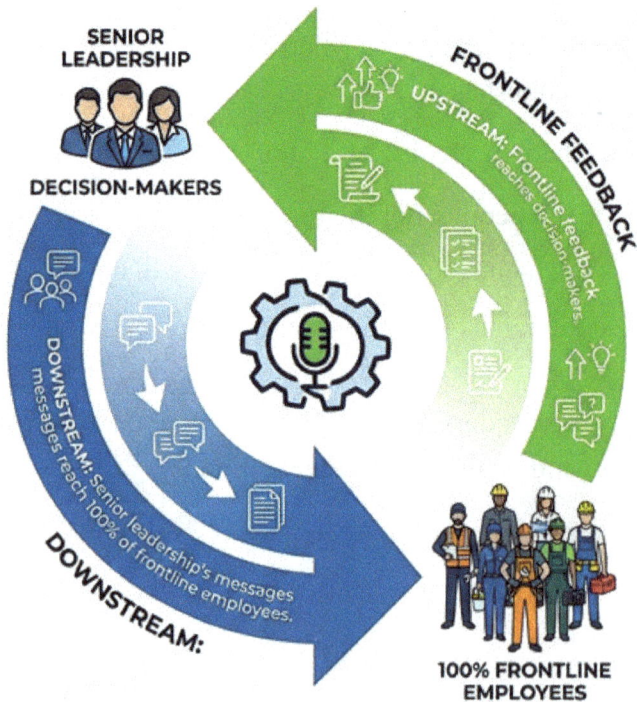

THE DAILY DIALOGUE
TWO-WAY COMMUNICATION CHANNEL

SENIOR LEADERSHIP

DECISION-MAKERS

FRONTLINE FEEDBACK

UPSTREAM: Frontline feedback reaches decision-makers

DOWNSTREAM: Senior leadership's messages reach 100% of frontline employees.

DOWNSTREAM:

100% FRONTLINE EMPLOYEES

Objective 3: Leader Confidence

An accidental leader walks into training nervous. They walk out with a cheat sheet, a process, and examples of what good looks like. But the real confidence doesn't come from the training itself. It comes three weeks later.

That's when they start seeing the data. Engagement scores tick up. Safety incidents drop. Quality metrics improve. Turnover starts to slow. The leader realizes this is actually working and that builds confidence.

The Coaching Loop

Training doesn't stop after the initial session. The Daily Dialogue methodology includes ongoing coaching, especially in remote rollouts.

Here's how it works:

Leaders are required to record their first few Daily Dialogues and send the videos to us for review. We give them tactical feedback such as:

- "You spent 22 minutes. Tighten it to 15."
- "Great question on that behavior. Do that more."
- "You let the conversation drift. Redirect to the board."

We watch the video, identify the gaps, and provide leaders with ways to fix them.

Tracking the Huddle

After each huddle, leaders log what happened. You can do this in a spreadsheet: date, who attended, what was discussed, any recognitions given, barometer results, improvement opportunities raised.

Or if you're using the Habit app, mark the huddle complete, and the data flows automatically. When employees scan the barometer QR code at the start of the huddle, their mood data appears instantly. Recognition gets logged in real-time. Improvement opportunities are captured with a few taps.

The app removes the administrative friction from tracking the Daily Dialogue. You get reports that show huddle completion rates, recognition patterns, mood trends, and improvement opportunity resolution, all without managing a spreadsheet.

From Setup to Execution

The board is the cheat sheet. The training is the instruction manual. But none of it matters until that first huddle actually happens.

Because here's the reality: most of your frontline leaders aren't going to become inspiring communicators. They're not going to give TED Talks. They're not going to be naturally charismatic.

But they can point at a board. They can ask a question. And they can follow a process.

And if they do that every single day, culture compounds.

The huddle is the deposit. Everything up to this point has been preparation. Now it's time to execute.

References and Citations:

[10] People Management. "'Accidental managers 'without proper leadership training contributing to almost one in three workers walking out, research finds." https://www.peoplemanagement.co.uk/article/1844443/acciden tal-managers-without-proper-leadership-training-contributing-almost-one-three-workers-walking-out-research-finds

[11] Fortune. "More than two-thirds of bosses are 'accidental managers'—and their requests for proper training are being ignored." https://fortune.com/2024/05/23/accidental-managers-no-training-losing-talent-survey/

CHAPTER 5

A - Appreciation

~~~

Your company probably has a recognition program. Employee of the Month. Service awards. Anniversary celebrations. Maybe a peer nomination system where people submit forms that nobody reads until the quarterly meeting.

And your turnover is still high. Morale is still mediocre. People still don't feel valued.

The difference between recognition that changes behavior and recognition that wastes time comes down to three things: specificity, timing, and frequency.

Most programs get all three wrong.

The Appreciation component of the Performance Habit system fixes this. By building recognition into the daily routine until it becomes automatic.

Daily, Specific, Public

Appreciation in the Performance Habit system happens during the Daily Dialogue. Every single day, in front of the team, for specific, observable behaviors.

Here's what that looks like:

"I want to recognize Marcus. Yesterday during the shipping crunch, I watched you notice we were running low on packing tape. Instead of waiting for someone to tell you, you grabbed backup supplies before we ran out. That's anticipating problems, not just reacting. Nice work."

Notice what just happened:

Specific. Not "Marcus is great." But "Marcus did this specific thing."

Timely. Yesterday. Not last month. Not "over the past quarter."

Behavioral. "Anticipating problems" ties directly to an observable behavior the team understands.

Public. Everyone hears it. Marcus feels seen. Others understand what "good" looks like. And it takes thirty seconds.

The goal isn't to recognize one person per month. It's to recognize at least one person per day. If you have a team of 20 and you're recognizing 1-2 people daily, everyone gets recognized multiple times per month. Nobody feels overlooked. Everyone gets feedback on what they're doing right.

That changes the dynamic entirely. Instead of scarcity (only one person matters), you create abundance (good work gets noticed consistently).

Peer-to-Peer Recognition

Top-down recognition matters. But peer-to-peer recognition matters more. [12]

When your supervisor recognizes you, it feels good. When your coworker recognizes you, it feels authentic.

Here's why: your peers see your work differently than your boss does. They notice the small things. The extra effort. The moment you helped when nobody else was watching. They know what the work actually requires because they do it too.

During the Daily Dialogue, after the leader recognizes someone, you open it up.

"Anyone else want to call out good work?"

At first, maybe nobody says anything. People aren't used to recognizing each other publicly. It feels awkward.

But after a few weeks, someone speaks up.

"I want to recognize Jennifer. Yesterday I was struggling with the new system and she stopped what she was doing to walk me through it. She didn't have to do that."

The leader writes it down. Logs it in the system. Jennifer gets recognized. And suddenly, peer recognition becomes part of the culture.

This creates something powerful: horizontal accountability and appreciation. People start looking for good work in their peers because they know it'll get called out. The culture shifts from "I do my job, you do yours" to "we're in this together."

Peer recognition also surfaces things leaders don't see. The quiet acts of help. The behind-the-scenes problem-solving. The emotional support during tough shifts. Leaders can't observe everything. But peers can.

When you combine top-down recognition (leader identifies behaviors) with peer-to-peer recognition (team acknowledges each other), you create a culture where appreciation flows in all directions.

The System Behind the Recognition

Here's where it gets interesting.

When you log recognition, it creates data. Who's getting recognized? For what behaviors? How often?

You can track this in a spreadsheet. Create columns: date, employee name, behavior recognized, who recognized them (leader or peer). Review it weekly. If Marcus has 5 recognitions and Carlos has zero, that's a flag. Either Carlos isn't doing recognition-worthy work (unlikely) or the leader isn't noticing his contributions (more likely).

Or, of course, you can use the Habit app.

After the Daily Dialogue, the leader logs each recognition into the app. Marcus got recognized for anticipating problems. Jennifer got recognized by a peer for helping with training. The app automatically generates a top 10 list of most recognized employees. The leader can see, at a glance, who hasn't been recognized lately.

The app turns recognition into visibility. It prevents the same three people from getting all the recognition while others feel invisible. It keeps leaders accountable without manual spreadsheet work.

This is where the system connects daily deposits to monthly outcomes.

At the end of each week, the data show which employee received the most recognitions. That person becomes Employee of the Week and receives a small reward like a $25 gift card.

At the end of each month, the employee with the most recognitions becomes Employee of the Month. They get a bigger perk, like a VIP parking spot and a $250 gift card. More importantly, they've been recognized 15-20 times that month for specific behaviors that drove results.

Everyone on the team knows exactly why that person earned it. They watched it happen. They heard the behaviors called out. There's no mystery. No politics.

And here's the real compound effect: those employees who consistently rack up recognitions become the natural candidates for promotion. Because you're not guessing who your top performers are. You have data on who demonstrates the behaviors you value, day after day.

This addresses one of the biggest drivers of turnover: lack of growth. When high performers see no path to advancement, they leave. When they see that consistent demonstration of valued behaviors leads to recognition, rewards, and eventually promotion, they stay.

That's Achievement (the A in BAR). And when people feel achievement regularly, they're 31% less likely to leave. [7]

Building the Habit

In the Performance Habit, appreciation is a habit you build.

During the Daily Dialogue, leaders recognize at least one person daily. They invite peer recognition. They log it in the Habit app after the huddle. They check the data to ensure nobody falls through the cracks.

Within 30 days, recognition becomes routine. Within 60 days, it becomes expected. Within 90 days, it becomes culture.

Employees start doing recognition-worthy work more intentionally because they know it'll be noticed. Peers start looking for good work because appreciation is part of the daily rhythm. Leaders stop forgetting to recognize because the board prompts them.

▶ Red Flag:

If you have an Employee of the Month program but couldn't name three specific behaviors your top performers demonstrated this week, your recognition is generic and ineffective. Fix the specificity problem first.

Reflection Questions

1. When was the last time you recognized someone on your team, and was it specific enough for them to know exactly what to repeat?

2. What percentage of your team has been recognized in the past 30 days?

3. If you asked your employees whether they feel appreciated, what would they say?

4. Are you creating scarcity (one person per month) or abundance (multiple people per day) in your recognition approach?

5. What would change if good work was acknowledged publicly every single day instead of waiting for the quarterly award ceremony?

References:

[7] BetterUp. "The Value of Belonging at Work: Investing in Workplace Inclusion." https://www.betterup.com/blog/the-value-of-belonging-at-work

[12] Forbes. "New Research Unlocks the Secret of Employee Recognition." https://www.forbes.com/sites/joshbersin/2012/06/13/new-research-unlocks-the-secret-of-employee-recognition/

CHAPTER 6

B - Barometer

(Mood Check)

~~≈~~

Most leaders find out their team is struggling when someone quits. By then, the frustration has been building for weeks. The disengagement has been spreading. The good employees have been updating their resumes. And you had no idea because nobody told you.

That's because most organizations measure morale once a year (if that) through an engagement survey that arrives six months after the data was collected, tells you what you already suspected, and provides zero actionable insight into what's happening right now.

The Barometer in the Performance Habit system fixes this by giving you a real-time read on team morale every single day before the huddle even starts.

It's simple, fast, and surprisingly effective. And it catches problems before they become resignations.

The QR Code Mood Check System

Here's how it works.

On the Daily Dialogue board, in the People section, there's a QR code. Every morning when employees arrive for the huddle, the first thing they do is pull out their phone, scan the code, and tap one of three faces:

- Smiley face: I'm doing great
- Neutral face: I'm so so
- Frowny face: I'm struggling

That's it. Three seconds.

Instantly, the team leader's app updates with the anonymous data. They can see at a glance: 12 people here today. 9 smileys. 2 neutrals. 1 frowny.

The employee also has the option to leave a comment if they want to expand. Most don't. But when someone does, it's usually because they need to be heard.

"Feeling overwhelmed with the new process."

"Dealing with a family emergency."

"Frustrated that the equipment keeps breaking."

The leader reads the mood data, then opens the huddle.

"Alright team, I see 9 of you are doing amazing today. That's great. However, 3 of you seem to be struggling. Does anyone want to share what's going on?"

Sometimes someone speaks up.

"My dog just died yesterday, so I'm having a rough time."

And just like that, the team knows. They offer sympathy. Someone shares a similar experience. Another person offers to cover the tougher tasks today. The employee feels seen, supported, and less alone.

That's social support. That's Belonging (the B in BAR). And it happens because you asked.

Other times, nobody says anything. The room stays quiet. People aren't ready to share publicly.

That's fine. The leader lets the team know:

"If anyone wants to talk privately, my door is always open. Come find me during break or after shift."

Later that day, one of the employees shows up.

"Hey, can I talk to you for a minute?"

And now the leader learns what's actually going on. Maybe it's a conflict with a coworker. Maybe it's a personal issue affecting focus. Maybe it's frustration with a policy that makes no sense.

Either way, the leader knows. And knowing gives them the chance to help before it becomes a resignation.

What to Do When the Barometer Drops

The Barometer isn't just about collecting data. It's about acting on it. Because the data are anonymous, you can't pull someone aside to ask what's going on. You can't see a trend within a specific person. This is the downside of anonymity, but it also creates psychological safety which builds trust. That said, you can invite people to seek you out and you can see trends for the team at large.

If you see three frowny faces, you open the floor for discussion during the huddle. Something's affecting multiple people. Surface it publicly and address it.

If you see eight frowny faces, you escalate. Something systemic is broken. A policy changed. A leader failed. A process collapsed. This points to a team-wide problem that requires immediate attention.

Here's what not to do: ignore it.

Leaders who track the Barometer but don't act on it do more harm than asking in the first place. Because now employees know you see their struggle and chose to do nothing about it.

Pattern Recognition: Spotting Issues Before They Escalate

The real power of the Barometer isn't in the daily snapshot. It's in the trend.

When you track mood daily, patterns emerge.

You notice that every Tuesday, mood drops. Why? Turns out Tuesday is when the most difficult client calls come in. Now you know to either staff heavier on Tuesdays or provide additional support.

You notice that the entire team's mood dropped suddenly over the course of three days. What changed? New policy? Leadership shift? Equipment failure? Something happened. Figure it out.

One organization tracked Barometer data across multiple teams. One team's mood dropped significantly over the span of a week. The consultant reviewed the data and called the leadership team.

"Did you replace the team leader recently?"

"Actually, yes. We brought in a rockstar from New York. Super experienced. Great credentials. Why?"

"Your rockstar is killing the team."

The executive was skeptical. "She's been doing great work. Very high standards."

"Check the data. Your team went from 85% positive mood to 40% in one week. That's not a coincidence. That's her."

They dug deeper. Turns out, the "rockstar" had high standards, but zero emotional intelligence. She criticized publicly, micromanaged constantly, and made people feel incompetent. Her technical skills were excellent. Her leadership skills were toxic.

They moved her out of the leadership role. Within a week, the team's mood shot back up.

Without the Barometer, they wouldn't have known until people started quitting. By then, they'd have lost good employees, damaged morale, and spent months rebuilding trust.

Instead, they caught it in seven days and fixed it before the damage spread.

That's the power of leading indicators. You see the fire when it's still a spark.

Tracking Mood Over Time

You can track the Barometer in a spreadsheet. Create columns for date, total team members present, number of smileys, neutrals, and frownies, and any comments. Calculate the percentage of positive responses daily. Review trends weekly.

Alternatively, when employees scan the QR code, the data flows into the Habit app instantly. The leader opens the huddle seeing real-time mood before they say a word. The app tracks trends over time automatically: this week versus last week, this month versus last month. It flags sudden drops. If you're tracking multiple teams or want to spot patterns across locations, the app does the math for you.

Why It Works

The Barometer works because it normalizes struggle.

In most workplaces, admitting you're having a tough day feels like weakness. So people pretend they're fine. They smile through frustration, hide exhaustion, and internalize stress until they burn out.

The Barometer says: it's okay to not be okay. We're asking because we care, not because we're judging.

When the leader opens the huddle and says, "*I see 3 of you are struggling today,*" it creates permission for honesty. Someone might not have volunteered that their dog died. But when the leader asks, they feel safe to share.

And when they share, the team responds with empathy. Because everyone's had a tough week. Everyone's dealt with personal loss. Everyone knows what it's like to show up when you'd rather stay home.

That's culture.

Reflection Questions

1. When was the last time you knew someone on your team was struggling before they quit or had a breakdown?

2. What would change if you had real-time visibility into morale instead of waiting for annual surveys?

3. Do your employees believe you care about their wellbeing, or do they think you just care about their productivity?

4. If someone on your team is having the worst week of their year, would they feel safe telling you, or would they hide it until they burn out?

CHAPTER 7

I - Improvement Opportunities

⁓

Most performance problems aren't motivation problems. They're resource problems.

When performance is down, it's easy to think your employees are lazy. But in fact, they may be working with broken equipment, outdated systems, unclear processes, or missing tools. They know exactly what would make their job easier, faster, and better. They just haven't been asked.

Or worse, they've been asked before, nothing changed, and now they don't bother speaking up.

The I in the Performance Habit system stands for Improvement Opportunities. It's the part of the Daily Dialogue where the leader asks one simple question:

"What do you need to do your job even better?"

That framing matters. Because it assumes people want to do great work. They just need the right resources to do it.

The Question Nobody Asks

Here's what happens in most organizations.

Leadership sets performance goals. "Increase productivity by 15%. Reduce errors by 10%. Improve customer satisfaction scores."

Then they measure whether those goals are met. And when they're not, they assume it's a people problem.

"The team isn't motivated."

"They're not working hard enough."

"We need better training."

So they bring in a consultant to run a workshop on accountability. Or they implement a new incentive program. Or they replace the manager.

And performance still doesn't improve.

Because the problem was never the people. The problem was that Maria has been walking to the 4th floor to get ice 12 times per shift for the past six months, and nobody thought to ask why.

Maria's Ice Machine

We got called into a hospital to work with their worst performing unit. The leadership team was frustrated. Metrics were down. Patient satisfaction was low. Turnover was climbing.

They pointed us to Maria. "She's the worst performer on the floor. We don't know what to do with her."

We talked to Maria.

Turns out, Maria wasn't a bad nurse. Maria was exhausted because every time a patient needed ice, she had to walk to the 4th floor, fill a container, and bring it back down. Twelve times per shift. Sometimes more.

We went to leadership. "Maria needs an ice machine on her floor."

"That's it? An ice machine?"

"That's it."

They got her an ice machine.

Within two weeks, Maria's performance metrics shot up. She went from worst performer to top performer on the unit.

Not because she suddenly became motivated. Not because someone gave her a pep talk. Because someone removed the obstacle that was killing her efficiency and morale.

That's the power of asking the right question and actually following through.

Why Leaders Don't Ask

If the solution is this simple, why don't more leaders do it?

Three reasons.

Reason 1: They assume they already know what the team needs. Leaders think they understand the frontline experience because they used to do the job. But things change. Processes evolve. New bottlenecks emerge. What worked five years ago doesn't work today. If you're not on the floor every day, you don't know what's actually happening.

Reason 2: They're afraid of opening the floodgates. "If I ask what they need, they'll ask for everything. I can't afford to say yes to every request."

So they don't ask at all. Which means they never find out about the $200 ice machine that would fix a $50,000 performance problem.

Reason 3: They've asked before and didn't follow through. The worst thing you can do is ask for input, collect a list of issues, and then do nothing. Because now your team knows you don't actually care about their input. You were just performing "engagement."

How It Works in the Daily Dialogue

At the end of every huddle, after recognition, after reviewing the Barometer, after discussing priorities, the leader asks:

"What do you need to do your job even better?"

Listen for it.

"The printer on our floor jams constantly. It takes 20 minutes to fix every time. Can we get it serviced?"

The leader writes it down. "Got it. I'll follow up with facilities today and let you know tomorrow what the timeline looks like."

The next day, during the huddle:

"Update on the printer. Facilities is sending someone Thursday morning to either fix it or replace it. Should be handled by end of week."

That's it. Issue raised. Action taken. Update provided.

The employee feels heard. The team sees that speaking up leads to results. Next time the question is asked, more people contribute.

"The schedule changes too late. We don't know our shifts until the night before."

"The safety gloves rip too easily. Can we try a different brand?"

"The loading dock light is out. It's hard to see when we're unloading at night."

None of these are massive requests. But each one affects performance, safety, or morale. And most of them are fixable if someone just knows about them.

The Follow-Up Is Everything

Asking the question is easy. Following through is what separates real leadership from performative leadership.

Here's the process:

Step 1: Capture the request during the huddle. Write it down. Log it. Don't trust your memory.

Step 2: Between huddles, take action. Talk to your manager. Submit the request to facilities. Research vendors. Get approval. Find out the timeline.

You don't need to solve it yourself. You need to move it forward.

Step 3: Provide an update at the next huddle. Even if the answer is no. Even if it's going to take three months. Even if you're still waiting for approval.

"Update on the safety gloves. I talked to procurement. They're testing a new brand next week and if it works, we'll switch over by end of month."

Or:

"Update on the schedule. I talked to the GM. She said the system doesn't allow us to post schedules earlier, but she's going to look into whether we can at least give you a two-day notice instead of one. I'll follow up next week."

Or:

"Update on the loading dock light. Facilities said it's not in this quarter's budget, but they'll add it to Q2. I pushed back and said it's a safety issue. Still waiting to hear if they'll move it up. I'll keep you posted."

Notice what just happened. Even when the answer isn't ideal, the leader communicated the status. The team knows their request didn't disappear into a black hole. Someone's actually working on it.

That builds trust. And trust is what keeps people raising issues instead of staying silent.

Tracking Improvement Opportunities

You can track improvement opportunities in a spreadsheet. Create columns for date raised, issue description, who raised it, status (open/in progress/completed), and date resolved. Review it weekly to ensure nothing falls through the cracks.

Or you can use the Habit app. When a leader logs an improvement opportunity, it goes into a central tracker. The app shows how many opportunities were raised, how many got completed, and how many are still outstanding. Leaders can update status with a tap. Executives can see resolution rates across teams. The data shows whether you're actually fixing problems or just collecting them.

The Compounding Effect of Small Fixes

Here's what most leaders miss: fixing small things creates massive momentum.

Maria's ice machine cost $200. It probably saved the hospital $50,000 in lost productivity, overtime, and eventual turnover.

The printer repair took one service call. It saved 20 minutes per day across a 10-person team. That's 200 minutes daily. Over a year, that's 1,200 hours of recovered productivity.

The loading dock light cost $80. It prevented a potential injury that could've cost $100,000 in workers' comp claims and lost time.

Small fixes compound. They improve performance, morale, and safety. They show employees that leadership is paying attention. They build trust.

But the biggest benefit isn't even the fix itself. It's the signal it sends.

When you ask for improvement opportunities and actually follow through, you're telling your team: your input matters. Your obstacles matter. Your experience matters.

And when people feel like they matter, they perform differently. Not because you incentivized them. Because you removed the barriers that were making their job unnecessarily hard.

What Gets Raised

The types of improvement opportunities that surface during Daily Dialogues fall into a few categories:

Equipment and Tools: "The forklift needs maintenance." "We need more headsets." "The chairs in the break room are falling apart."

Process Issues: "The approval process for overtime takes too long." "We're filling out the same form three times in different systems." "The handoff between shifts isn't clear."

Communication Gaps: "We don't know when corporate decisions get made until they affect us." "The email updates don't reach the people on the floor." "We need earlier notice when schedules change."

Safety Concerns: "The walkway gets icy and nobody salts it." "The ventilation in the back isn't working." "We need better lighting in the parking lot."

Training Needs: "Nobody showed us how to use the new system." "We need a refresher on the safety protocols." "New hires aren't getting enough shadowing time."

Most of these aren't expensive or complicated, but most go unaddressed because nobody's asking the question consistently.

⚡ Quick Win:

Tomorrow at your team meeting, ask: "What is preventing you from doing an even better job?" Write down every response. Pick one thing you can act on immediately. Report back the next day with an update. Do that for five days in a row. Watch what happens.

🚩 Red Flag:

If you've asked for improvement opportunities in the past but can't name three specific things you followed up on, your team doesn't trust you. Stop asking until you're ready to actually follow through. Asking without acting is worse than not asking at all.

Reflection Questions

1. When was the last time you asked your team what they need, and how many of those requests did you actually follow up on?

2. If you asked your team right now what's making their job harder than it should be, what would they say?

3. How many performance problems on your team are actually resource problems in disguise?

4. What's the Maria's ice machine story in your organization - the simple fix that nobody's made because nobody's asked?

5. Do your employees believe that speaking up leads to change, or have they learned that silence is safer than honesty?

CHAPTER 8

T - Tracking

～

You can't manage what you don't measure. That's the cliché. And like most clichés, it's true because people keep ignoring it.

Most organizations collect mountains of data: Revenue, turnover, customer satisfaction scores, productivity metrics, error rates. But they're measuring outcomes, not inputs. They're tracking what happened, not what's happening.

By the time the data shows a problem, the damage is done. Employees have quit. Customers have complained. Performance has tanked. And leadership is left asking, "*Why didn't we see this coming?*"

You didn't see it coming because you were watching the scoreboard instead of watching the game.

The T in the Performance Habit system stands for Tracking. Not tracking everything. Tracking the things that matter. The inputs that drive outputs. The leading indicators that predict lagging indicators. The daily behaviors that compound into long-term results.

When you track the right things, you don't just measure performance. You create it.

What We Track

The Performance Habit system tracks five categories of data, all pulled from the Daily Dialogue and logged in the app:

1. HUDDLE COMPLETION

Did the leader conduct the Daily Dialogue today? Yes or no. Simple.

This matters because the entire system collapses if huddles don't happen. If a leader skips two huddles in a week, that's a red flag. If a department hasn't logged a huddle in five days, leadership knows immediately that something's broken.

In organizations with multiple departments, this visibility is critical. You can see at a glance which teams are executing and which teams are drifting. No more guessing. No more excuses.

2. RECOGNITION DATA

Who got recognized? How many times? For what behaviors?

The system tracks the top 10 most-recognized employees across the organization. Not to create competition, but to create visibility.

When you see that Marcus has been recognized 12 times this month and Carlos hasn't been recognized once, you know something's off. Either Carlos isn't performing, or his leader isn't noticing. Either way, it's actionable.

When you track who's getting recognized consistently for the behaviors you value, those people become your natural promotion candidates. You're not guessing who your top performers are. You have data.

3. IMPROVEMENT OPPORTUNITIES

How many improvement requests were made? How many have been resolved? How many are still pending?

This data keeps leaders accountable. If a team raises 15 improvement opportunities and only 2 get addressed, you know follow-through is a problem. If another team raises 15 opportunities and 13 get resolved, you know that leader is executing.

The data also surface systemic issues. If five different teams are all requesting better equipment, that's not a team problem. That's an organizational problem. Aggregate the data, escalate it to senior leadership, and make the case for investment.

Tracking improvement opportunities also prevents requests from disappearing. When someone raises an issue, it gets logged. The leader can't forget about it.

4. BAROMETER (MOOD DATA)

What's the team's mood today? This week? This month?

Mood tracked over time creates a trend line for each team. You can see whether morale is rising, falling, or holding steady.

This is one of your most powerful leading indicators. When mood drops, performance follows. When frustration builds, turnover follows. The Barometer gives you early warning.

5. CUSTOMER SATISFACTION (OPTIONAL)

If you give customers a QR code to scan, you can track their satisfaction in real time. The data create a color-coded bar graph showing satisfaction trends with any comments they provided. You can spot service issues before they become complaints.

How to Track It

You have two options.

OPTION 1: SPREADSHEET TRACKING

Create a simple tracking system with these tabs:

- Daily Huddle Log (Date, Team, Leader, Completed Y/N)
- Recognition Tracker (Date, Employee Name, Behavior, Recognized By)
- Improvement Opportunities (Date Raised, Issue, Status, Date Resolved)
- Barometer Results (Date, Smileys, Neutrals, Frownies, Percentage Positive)
- Customer Feedback (if applicable)

Update it daily. Review it weekly. Calculate monthly trends. This works. It requires discipline and admin time, but it works.

OPTION 2: HABIT APP

The app automates everything described above. Leaders log huddles with a tap. Recognition flows in as it happens. Improvement opportunities get tracked with status updates. Barometer data appear instantly when employees scan the QR code. Customer satisfaction graphs update in real time.

The Monthly Report

At the end of each month, the system generates a report. This is a focused summary of what matters:

- Huddle completion rate by team

- Top 10 most-recognized employees
- Mood trends by department
- Improvement opportunities: raised, resolved, pending
- Customer satisfaction trends (if tracking)

The report goes to senior leadership with specific recommendations:

"Department A has had declining mood for three weeks. We recommend leadership check-in."

"Department B has 18 unresolved improvement opportunities. We recommend escalation to operations."

The report turns data into action. It tells leaders what's working, what's broken, and what to do about it.

And over time, it tells a story. You can see whether the system is driving results. You can prove ROI. You can show correlation between daily behaviors and long-term outcomes.

Proof Across Industries

We've implemented the Performance Habit system in hospitals, airports, call centers, fast food, retail, mining, forestry, and laboratories.

Different industries. Different challenges. Different metrics.

But the pattern is the same: when you implement the system, outcomes improve.

In hospitals, patient experience scores go up. In airports, on-time performance improves. In call centers, customer satisfaction increases. In fast food, speed of service and order accuracy get better. In retail, employee engagement and sales per employee climb. In mining and forestry, safety incidents drop.

⚡ Quick Win:

Pick one metric from the Performance Habit system and start tracking it this week. Huddle completion. Recognition frequency. Mood. Anything. Log it every day for five days. At the end of the week, review the data and ask: what does this tell me? Then act on it.

🚩 Red Flag:

If you're tracking data but not reviewing it, you're wasting time. Data without action is just noise. If you haven't looked at your team's metrics in two weeks, stop tracking until you're ready to actually use the information.

Reflection Questions

1. What are you currently tracking, and is it telling you what's happening or what already happened?

2. If you could see one piece of real-time data about your team every day, what would you want to know?

3. When was the last time data revealed a problem before it became a crisis?

4. Do you know who your top performers are based on evidence, or are you guessing based on visibility and favoritism?

5. If your team's mood has been declining for two weeks, would you know? And if you knew, what would you do about it?

CHAPTER 9

The Launch Blueprint

~

M ost culture initiatives fail because they skip preparation and jump straight to execution.

Leaders announce the new program on Monday. By Tuesday, frontline supervisors are expected to run perfect meetings with tools they've never seen, using a process nobody explained, tracking metrics nobody defined. By Friday, it's chaos. By Week 3, it's abandoned.

The Performance Habit system doesn't fail because we don't start with execution. We start with architecture.

By the time the first Daily Dialogue happens, the foundation is built. The structure is clear. The tools are ready. Leaders know exactly what to do.

There's no guessing. No improvising. No "we'll figure it out as we go."

Stage 1: Discovery and Design

Before we build anything, we need to understand what we're building for.

We sit down with senior leadership and map the organization. Not the org chart on the website, but the real structure: Who actually runs things, where decisions get made, which departments are thriving and which are struggling?

We ask questions most consultants skip:

ORGANIZATIONAL STRUCTURE

- What does your leadership hierarchy look like from C-Suite to frontline?
- How many departments, locations, and teams do you have?
- Who owns quality, operations, training, or continuous improvement?

STRATEGIC PRIORITIES

- Which department is struggling the most right now?
- What outcomes are you trying to move? Safety? Turnover? Customer satisfaction? Productivity?
- What have you already tried, and why didn't it work?

ROLLOUT APPROACH

- Do you want to pilot with one department or roll out across the organization?
- If you're piloting, which department should we start with?
- Who internally will own this after we leave?

If you want to start with your worst-performing department (which we recommend), we focus there. Prove it works where it's hardest, and the rest of the organization will follow.

If leadership wants to go all-in immediately, we structure a phased rollout so we don't overwhelm the system or dilute the training.

The critical decision at this stage: who's going to own this internally?

Most organizations have someone responsible for quality, continuous improvement, operations, or training. That person becomes the internal champion. They're the bridge between us and the frontline. They'll monitor data, escalate issues, train new leaders, and ensure the system survives after we're gone.

If no one like that exists, we work directly with frontline leaders. Either way, someone internal has to own it. Culture initiatives die without internal ownership.

Stage 2: System Architecture

Once we understand the structure, we build the system.

This is where abstract concepts like "culture" and "engagement" turn into concrete tools, processes, and data structures.

BUILDING THE TRACKING INFRASTRUCTURE

If you're using the Habit app, we set up the department. That means:

- Loading every employee by name, role, and shift into the system
- Creating team hierarchies so leaders see only their team's data
- Generating unique Barometer QR codes for each department
- Setting permissions so frontline leaders access dashboards but can't see other teams' data

If you're tracking with spreadsheets, we create the templates you'll use and train someone to maintain them.

DEFINING THE RULES OF THE GAME

This is where we turn vague corporate values into observable behaviors.

Most organizations have values posted on the wall or their website. Integrity. Respect. Excellence. Teamwork. Great words. Zero practical impact.

We make them real.

We ask leadership: "What values do you want your culture built on?"

They give us the list. Then we turn each value into 3-5 observable behaviors. Specific actions anyone can see, do, or recognize.

Value: Safety

- I always perform hand hygiene as appropriate
- I speak up when I see an unsafe condition
- I follow lockout/tagout procedures every time
- I report near-misses immediately
- I wear required PPE without being remin

Value: Respect

- I make eye contact when someone is speaking to me
- I clean up after myself in shared spaces
- I address people by name
- I listen without interrupting
- I assume positive intent before reacting

Value: Accountability

- I show up on time, ready to work
- I follow through on commitments I make
- I own my mistakes instead of blaming others
- I communicate when I need help before it becomes a crisis
- I complete tasks without being reminded

Value: Teamwork

- I help others when I finish my work early
- I share information that helps the team succeed
- I ask "what do you need?" instead of waiting to be asked
- I step in when someone is overwhelmed
- I give credit to others who contributed

Value: Customer Focus

- I greet every customer within 30 seconds
- I follow up on commitments I make to customers
- I take ownership of problems instead of passing them off
- I communicate delays proactively
- I ask for feedback on how we can improve

We typically create 15-30 observable behaviors across all values. These rotate on a calendar during the Daily Dialogue so the team discusses one each day. By the end of the month, they've cycled through all of them at least once. Then we start again.

DESIGNING THE BOARD

Now we design the Daily Dialogue board and customize it with the client's official colors, logo, and branding.

The board includes:

- Purpose statement (why the organization exists)
- Core values
- Observable behaviors (rotating calendar)
- Barometer QR code
- Company news section
- KPI/metrics section
- Space for improvement opportunities

We design it digitally, get approval from leadership, and then the client prints it (usually 6'x4') and mounts it on the wall where the team gathers for Daily Dialogues.

By the end of this stage, the infrastructure is complete. App loaded. Behaviors defined. Board designed. Now we train.

Stage 3: Training and Onboarding

We don't train every frontline leader individually. That doesn't scale.

Instead, we use a train-the-trainer model when possible.

We identify 1-3 internal champions (usually from quality, operations, or training) and train them on:

- **The methodology**: Why Daily Dialogues work, the science of repetition, the three motivators (Belonging, Relevance, Achievement)

- **The board**: How to read it, how to follow it, how to guide others through it

- **The app**: How to log data, how to review dashboards, how to track trends

- **Coaching techniques**: How to give feedback, how to tighten a 20-minute huddle into 15, how to encourage peer recognition

By the end, internal champions should be able to train a frontline leader, review a recorded huddle, and provide actionable feedback.

If the organization doesn't have internal champions or prefers direct support, we train frontline leaders ourselves. Either way, the training follows the same structure.

THE TRAINING SESSION

Training includes five components:

- **The methodology**: The "why" behind the Performance Habit

- **Board walkthrough**: How to follow the board for the Daily Dialogue

- **Video examples**: Visual modeling of how to run the Daily Dialogue

- **Practice and coaching**: Leaders practice standing in front of the board and rehearse the flow. They're coached on common mistakes:

- "You turned your back to the team. Face them, not the board."

- "You're reading the values word-for-word. Point to them and ask the team what they mean instead."

- "You forgot to open it up for peer recognition. That's critical."

- "You spent too long on KPIs. State the number, connect it to behavior, move on."

- 5. **Tracking training**: Leaders get trained on the tracking system.

How to:

- Review Barometer data at the start of the huddle
- Log recognition after the huddle (who, for what behavior)
- Track improvement opportunities and update status
- Review team dashboards to spot trends

Stage 4: Data Review and Iteration

While leaders are executing, we're monitoring data.

We review dashboards weekly and look for patterns:

- Huddle compliance
- Recognition frequency
- Mood trends
- Improvement opportunity resolution

The data drive action. It tells leaders what's working, what's broken, and what to do about it.

Stage 5: Scale and Sustain

Once the first department is executing consistently, we expand.

We use the same blueprint: map the structure, build the system, define the behaviors, train the leaders, launch with coaching, monitor the data.

But now it's faster because the internal champions know the process. They can train new leaders. They can review videos. They can troubleshoot issues without external help.

That's how you scale. Not by making the organization dependent on consultants, but by building internal capability.

What Success Looks Like

Within 60-90 days of launch, you should see measurable change:

- Huddle compliance above 90%
- Recognition frequency where most employees are recognized multiple times per month
- Mood stable or improving
- Improvement opportunities being resolved at 50%+ rate
- Early correlation with key outcomes (safety, customer satisfaction, productivity)

Within six months, the culture starts to shift. Because these daily deposits compound over time.

⚡ Quick Win:

If you're planning to implement the Performance Habit system, start by mapping your structure this week. Who's on your leadership team? Who are your frontline leaders? Which department struggles the most? Who internally could own this? Answer those questions before you design a single board.

▶ Red Flag:

If you're thinking about launching without defining observable behaviors, training the leaders, or preparing the app, you're setting yourself up for failure. The preparation phase isn't optional. It's the foundation. Skip it, and the system collapses within weeks.

Reflection Questions

1. If you launched a Daily Dialogue tomorrow with no preparation, what would go wrong?

2. Can you name three observable behaviors for each of your core values right now, or are your values just words on a wall?

3. Do you have someone internal who could own this system, or would you be dependent on external support forever?

4. What's stopping you from starting with your worst-performing department?

5. Are you willing to invest time in preparation to ensure long-term success, or do you need to see results immediately even if it means the system fails in 30 days?

CHAPTER 10

Making It Stick

≈

Most culture initiatives are hard to launch and even harder to sustain. You spend months planning. Weeks training. The launch goes well. Then three months later, it's dead. Leaders got busy. People forgot. The system required too much manual effort to track, so tracking stopped. And once tracking stopped, accountability vanished.

With the Performance Habit, the launch takes the most prep work. But once it's launched, sustainability becomes easy because the system runs through an app that tracks everything automatically.

You don't have to chase people for compliance. The data show you who's executing and who's not. You don't have to guess whether the culture is improving. The metrics tell you in real time. You don't have to manually compile reports. The system generates them.

The hard work happens upfront. After that, the system sustains itself.

The System Runs Itself

Here's what sustainability looks like in practice:

Daily: Frontline leaders conduct 15-minute Daily Dialogues. Employees scan the Barometer. Leaders log data. Everything gets captured.

Weekly: The system owner (internal champion) reviews dashboards for compliance, mood, and recognition trends. They flag issues, follow up with leaders who are drifting, and identify the Employee of the Week.

Monthly: Reports get generated from the app. Senior leadership reviews the data. Feedback gets provided. Course corrections happen. And someone gets recognized and rewarded for becoming Employee of the Month.

Why Most Systems Die

Culture initiatives fail for predictable reasons:

Tracking requires too much effort. If logging data takes 20 minutes of manual work per leader per day, it won't happen consistently. Make it fast or it dies.

Nobody reviews the data. If you're collecting data but not reviewing it, leaders learn their compliance doesn't matter. What gets measured but ignored gets abandoned.

There's no accountability. If a leader skips huddles for two weeks and nothing happens, other leaders notice. The standard becomes optional. Within a month, compliance collapses.

The system owner leaves. If one person owns it and they quit, get promoted, or move departments, the system often dies with them. You need redundancy.

How to Keep It Alive

1. MAKE TRACKING FAST

If you're using spreadsheets, simplify them ruthlessly. Five minutes to log a huddle maximum. If it takes longer, leaders will skip it.

If you're using the Habit app, it's already fast. Leaders log huddles with a tap. The system does the rest.

Either way, reduce friction. The easier it is to comply, the more people will.

2. REVIEW DATA RELIGIOUSLY

Schedule a 30-minute standing weekly meeting. Have the system owner review the following:

- Huddle compliance by leader
- Recognition frequency
- Mood trends
- Improvement opportunity resolution rates

If compliance drops below 80%, find out why. If mood tanks on a specific team, investigate. If improvement opportunities aren't getting resolved, escalate.

The data tell you what's broken before it becomes a crisis.

3. HOLD LEADERS ACCOUNTABLE

If a leader consistently skips huddles, have the conversation:

"Your compliance is at 60%. What's blocking you?"

Maybe they don't understand the board. Maybe they're overwhelmed. Maybe they don't believe it matters.

Fix the blocker or replace the leader. You can't let non-compliance become acceptable.

4. BUILD REDUNDANCY

Train multiple people on the system. Don't let it live in one person's head. Document the process. Record training videos. Create a playbook.

When the original champion leaves, someone else steps in without missing a beat.

5. CONNECT BEHAVIORS TO OUTCOMES

Every quarter, show leadership the correlation:

"Since we started Daily Dialogues, turnover dropped from 82% to 45%. Mood scores improved 23%. Customer satisfaction is up 12%."

When people see the ROI, they protect the system. When they don't, they let it drift.

⚡ Quick Win:

If you're already running Daily Dialogues, pull up your compliance data right now. Which leaders are above 90%? Which are below 70%? Pick the lowest performer and have a conversation this week. "What's blocking you, and how do I help?" That's how you sustain.

🚩 Red Flag:

If you haven't reviewed your Performance Habit data in 30 days, your system is drifting. The data exists. The dashboards are there. You've got to manage the system, so if you haven't done so already, schedule your data review now.

Reflection Questions

1. Do you know your team's huddle compliance rate right now, or are you assuming it's fine because nobody's complaining?

2. When was the last time you reviewed mood trend data, and if the answer is "never," how would you know if morale is collapsing?

3. If a leader on your team has been skipping Daily Dialogues for two weeks, would you know?

4. Are you treating the Performance Habit system like a program (check in occasionally) or a system (review data monthly and act on what it tells you)?

5. If you had to prove to your board that this system is working, could you pull up data that shows correlation between daily behaviors and business outcomes?

CHAPTER 11

Common Objections

(And How to Answer Them)

⌠⌡

I've heard every objection. Some are legitimate questions from leaders who want to understand before committing. Others are excuses disguised as concerns. The difference is whether you're looking for reasons it might work or reasons it won't.

Here's how to tell: legitimate questions lead to implementation adjustments. Excuses lead to doing nothing.

If you're reading this chapter looking for permission to skip the work, close the book. You're not ready.

But if you're genuinely wrestling with how this fits your situation, these answers will help.

"We Don't Have 15 Minutes Every Day"

This is the most common objection. It's also the wrong calculation.

You're not choosing between fifteen minutes and nothing. You're choosing between **time now** or **money later**.

You don't have fifteen minutes for a Daily Dialogue, but you have:

- Weeks of lost productivity when someone mentally checks out
- Tens of thousands to replace them when they leave

- Management hours spent in exit interviews, coverage gaps, and damage control

Let's be concrete.

Fifteen minutes a day is 75 minutes a week.

Replacing one employee costs anywhere from **50–200% of their salary**, depending on role, ramp-up time, and mistakes along the way.

One supervisor told me, "I don't have time for daily huddles. I'm too busy managing problems."

Over three days, he spent six hours dealing with issues that would have surfaced in a short daily check-in. A safety concern. A scheduling miss. A morale issue that turned into call-outs.

Six hours of reactive leadership. All of it preventable.

Here's the real choice.

You will pay either way.

- Time upfront to align, recognize, and surface issues early
- Or money on the backend through turnover, disengagement, and constant rework

Pick your poison.

The Daily Dialogue doesn't add work. It reduces the most expensive kind. The kind you pretend is just "part of the job," until it shows up on your P&L.

If fifteen minutes feels impossible, that's not a scheduling problem. That's a leadership cost you're already paying for.

"Our People Won't Track Data"

This objection usually comes from leaders who assume their team can't or won't engage with any tracking system.

Let's address the core concern: can your team handle simple data collection?

The barometer scan takes five seconds. Pull out your phone, scan the QR code, tap a button. Green, yellow, or red. Done.

If your people can text, they can scan a QR code. If they truly don't have smartphones, have a tablet at the huddle location. They scan as they walk in. Same five seconds.

Or start with paper. Green sticky note, yellow sticky note, red sticky note. They put one in a box. You count them. Not elegant, but it works until you're ready for digital.

The tracking isn't the system. The tracking supports the system. The system is the Daily Dialogue, the recognition, the barometer check, the improvement opportunities. The tracking just makes it measurable.

But here's the real issue: if your concern is "we've tried tracking before and nobody did it," that's about accountability, not capability.

Tracking fails when it's complicated, when it doesn't matter to anyone, or when leadership doesn't use the data.

If you're asking frontline supervisors to track their dialogues but executives never look at the reports, it becomes pointless paperwork. But if executives review data weekly and coach based on what they see, suddenly it matters.

Whether you're using spreadsheets or an app, the principle is the same: make it simple, make it relevant, and make it visible. If those three things are true, tracking happens naturally.

"This Is Just Flavor-of-the-Month"

This objection usually comes from organizations that have launched and abandoned multiple initiatives over the years.

Lean, Six Sigma, Agile, employee engagement platforms, culture transformation programs. Each one was introduced with fanfare, required training, demanded new behaviors, and then quietly disappeared six months later when leadership got distracted by the next shiny object.

Your employees are tired. They've learned that "this too shall pass." So when you introduce the Performance Habit, they roll their eyes and think, "Here we go again."

That's fair.

The question is: are they right?

If you're treating this like another program that checks the box and dies then yes, this will be flavor-of-the-month. It'll fail like everything else.

But if you're treating this like a system that you embed into daily operations, that holds leaders accountable, and that you track, it won't be a program. It'll be how you operate.

Here's the difference:

Programs are additive. They sit on top of everything else you're doing. They require extra effort. They compete for attention. They fade when something more urgent appears.

Systems are integrative. They replace how you're already operating. They don't add work. They restructure it. They persist because they become the way things get done.

Are you willing to do this for 90 days without wavering? Are you willing to hold leaders accountable when they skip dialogues? Are you willing to make this non-negotiable instead of optional?

If yes, it's not flavor-of-the-month. It's culture change.

If no, don't start. Because one more failed initiative will make the next one even harder to launch.

"We Already Do Huddles"

Great. What are you covering in them?

Nine times out of ten, the answer is: "Production numbers from yesterday. Issues we're dealing with. Schedule changes."

That's a status update, not a Daily Dialogue.

If your huddles don't include purpose, recognition, barometer checks, and improvement opportunities, you're missing the entire cultural component. You're covering operations but ignoring people.

Most huddles are transactional. The Daily Dialogue is relational.

Here's the test: can your team recite your purpose statement? When was the last time someone was recognized publicly during a huddle? Do you know how your team is feeling today before the dialogue starts? Are you systematically capturing and resolving improvement opportunities?

If the answer to any of those is no, you're not doing Daily Dialogues. You're doing meetings.

The structure, the content, and the consistency all matter.

"We already do huddles" usually means "we already gather sometimes to talk about work stuff." That's not the same thing.

A Daily Dialogue happens at the same time every day, follows the same structure, covers people and performance (not just operations), and gets tracked. If yours doesn't do all of these, you don't already do this.

The good news? You're closer than most. You already have the habit of gathering. You just need to upgrade the content and structure.

That's easier than starting from scratch. But don't confuse "we already gather" with "we're already building culture systematically." Those are different things.

"Our Culture Is Fine"

This is the most dangerous objection because it's rooted in either ignorance or denial.

Let's test it.

What's your voluntary turnover rate? If it's above 20%, your culture isn't fine. You're losing one in five people annually by choice. That's not fine. That's expensive and unsustainable.

What's your employee engagement score? [13][8] If it's below 70%, your culture isn't fine. Thirty percent of your workforce is checked out. That shows up in quality, safety, and customer experience.

When was the last time you asked your frontline employees how they're feeling? Not through an annual survey six months ago. Today. This week. Do you know?

If you can't answer these questions with data, you don't know if your culture is fine. You're guessing. And leader perception of culture is consistently 20-30 points higher than employee perception.[9]

You think it's fine because nobody's complaining to your face. Meanwhile, they're complaining to each other, to their families, and to recruiters.

Here's the reality: if your culture were truly fine, you wouldn't be reading a book about retention and performance improvement. Something brought you here. Either turnover, engagement scores, productivity concerns, or a nagging sense that things could be better.

"Our culture is fine" is often code for "I don't want to admit we have a problem" or "I don't want to do the work."

Both are understandable human reactions. Neither is a strategy.

Even if your culture is fine by industry standards, the goal isn't to be fine. The goal is to be excellent. Fine is average. Average loses people to companies that are excellent.

The real question isn't "Is our culture fine?" It's "Could our culture be better?"

If the answer is yes (and it always is) then you have work to do.

The Performance Habit isn't a crisis intervention. It's a compounding system. It works when culture is broken. It also works when culture is fine but you want it to be great.

Don't wait for your culture to break. Invest in it while it's fine so it becomes exceptional.

The Meta-Objection: "This Seems Too Simple"

This isn't usually stated directly, but it underlies a lot of resistance.

The thinking goes: if culture change were this simple—five habits, fifteen minutes a day—everyone would be doing it. Since everyone isn't doing it, it must not work. Or there must be something more complex we're missing.

This logic is backwards.

Everyone isn't doing it because simple doesn't feel important. Leaders want complexity because complexity feels like sophistication. A 200-slide culture transformation deck feels more substantial than "do five things every day for fifteen minutes."

But complexity is the enemy of execution.

The reason most culture initiatives fail isn't because they're too simple. It's because they're too complicated. Nobody can remember twelve priorities, eight values, and fifteen new behaviors. So nothing changes.

The Performance Habit works because it's simple enough to remember and specific enough to execute.

Don't confuse simplicity with ineffectiveness. The most powerful systems are often the simplest. Compound interest is simple. It also builds wealth. Daily exercise is simple. It also transforms health.

Daily deposits are simple. They also transform culture.

The Real Question

Behind every objection is the same question: "Is this worth the effort?"

The answer depends on what you value.

If you value looking busy over being effective, skip this. The Performance Habit won't help you.

If you value checking boxes over changing outcomes, skip this. You can find cheaper ways to feel good about "investing in culture."

But if you value retention, engagement, performance, and sustainability, the question isn't whether this is worth it. The question is whether you can afford not to do it.

You're already spending the time managing turnover, putting out fires, and dealing with disengagement. You're already spending the money replacing people who leave. You're already losing productivity from teams that don't feel valued.

The real objection isn't time, technology, skepticism, or satisfaction.

The real objection is change.

Change is uncomfortable. It requires consistency. It demands accountability. It makes current failures visible.

That's hard.

But it's also the only path forward.

You can keep doing what you're doing and hope for different results. Or you can make the daily deposit and watch the compound effect take hold.

The choice is yours.

⚡ Quick Win:

Pick your biggest objection from this chapter. Write down one specific action you could take this week to test whether the objection is valid or just resistance. If it's time, track how you actually spend your day. If it's technology, have three employees test the barometer on their phones. If it's skepticism, commit to 30 days before evaluating. Test it. Don't assume it.

▶ Red Flag:

If you found yourself nodding along to multiple objections and thinking "yes, but our situation is different," you're not looking for solutions. You're looking for permission to stay stuck. That's a choice. Just be honest about it.

Reflection Questions

1. Which objection resonates most with you, and is it a legitimate concern or an excuse?

2. What would have to be true for you to commit to 90 days of consistent execution before evaluating results?

3. If your best employee told you they felt invisible and were thinking of leaving, would "we don't have time for daily dialogues" still feel like a valid objection?

4. What's the real cost of not doing this—in turnover dollars, lost productivity, and team morale—over the next 12 months?

5. Are you willing to be uncomfortable for 90 days to create a culture that compounds for years?

Chapter 12 References:

[13] Gallup. "State of the Global Workplace Report."
https://www.gallup.com/workplace/349484/state-of-the-global-
workplace.aspx

[8] Gallup. "How to Improve Employee Engagement in the
Workplace."
https://www.gallup.com/workplace/285674/improve-employee-
engagement-workplace.aspx

[9] Gallup. "State of the American Manager: Analytics and Advice
for Leaders." https://www.gallup.com/workplace/231593/state-
american-manager-report.aspx

CHAPTER 12

Your First Daily Deposit

〜

You've read the case for daily deposits. You understand the compound effect. You know the five HABIT components. You've confronted the objections.

Now comes the part that matters: doing it.

Self-Assessment: Where Are You Starting?

Before you begin, assess your current state honestly. I'm not here to judge. I just want you to know your baseline so you can measure progress.

Answer the questions about your team or knowing what you know about your company's management style. Rate each statement on a scale of 1-5 (1 = Never, 5 = Always):

DAILY ALIGNMENT

1. My team knows what's expected of them each day before they start work. ___

2. We have a consistent time and place where the team aligns daily. ___

3. People rarely ask me questions that should have been covered in a team meeting. ___

RECOGNITION

4. I recognize at least 2-3 people per week for specific behaviors. ___

5. Employees can describe what good work looks like because they've seen it acknowledged. ___

6. Peer-to-peer recognition happens regularly without prompting. ___

MORALE AWARENESS

7. I know how my team is feeling on any given day. ___

8. People tell me when they're struggling before it becomes a crisis. ___

9. I can predict who's at risk of leaving based on observable patterns. ___

IMPROVEMENT

10. My team feels comfortable raising obstacles without fear of blame. ___

11. When someone mentions a problem, it gets tracked and resolved. ___

12. We systematically remove friction that prevents people from doing their best work. ___

ACCOUNTABILITY

13. I track my leadership behaviors (dialogues, recognition, check-ins) consistently. ___

14. My manager can see data on how I'm building culture, not just outcomes. ___

15. I can show evidence of daily deposits, not just hope they're happening. ____

SCORING:

60-75: You're already operating at a high level. The Performance Habit will help you sustain and scale what's working.

45-59: You're inconsistent. You do some of these things sometimes. The system will give you structure to do them always.

30-44: You're reactive. You're managing problems, not preventing them. The daily deposit approach will shift you from firefighting to leading.

15-29: You're in crisis mode. Culture-building feels impossible because you're drowning. Start with one component. Prove to yourself it's possible. Then add the next one.

This assessment isn't about shame. It's about honesty. You can't improve what you won't acknowledge.

Next Steps and Resources

IF YOU'RE AN EXECUTIVE

You understand the system. You're convinced it's worth implementing. Here's how to bring it to your organization:

Step 1: Pilot with one location or team

Don't roll this out enterprise-wide on day one. Pick one location, one shift, or one department. Train those leaders. Implement the full Performance Habit system. Track everything.

Prove it works in your environment with your people before scaling.

Step 2: Measure and document

Track the inputs: How many daily dialogues happened? How many people were recognized? How many improvement opportunities were captured and resolved?

Track the outputs: What happened to turnover? Engagement scores? Safety incidents? Quality metrics?

Document the story. Not just the numbers, but the qualitative shifts. What did leaders say? What did employees say?

Step 3: Scale systematically

Once you have proof from the pilot, expand. One location at a time. Train leaders. Implement the board. Coach through the first 30 days.

Don't rush this. Slow, consistent rollout beats fast, sloppy execution every time.

If You Need Help

You can implement this yourself using this book as a guide. Many organizations do.

But if you want support (customizing the board, training leaders, coaching through implementation, setting up the Habit app), we can help.

We've implemented this system across industries: manufacturing, healthcare, logistics, hospitality, construction. The principles are universal. We customize it to your company, your mission statement, your desired results.

If you want to explore working together, visit www.turnkeyretention.com. We'll assess your situation, recommend a starting point, and build a plan that fits your organization.

But whether you work with us or do this yourself, the key is starting.

HOW TO BRING THIS TO YOUR ORGANIZATION

Let's say you're not the CEO. You're a mid-level manager, an HR leader, or a supervisor who sees the value but doesn't control the budget or strategy.

How do you get organizational buy-in?

Step 1: Start Where You Are

You don't need permission to do a Daily Dialogue with your team. You don't need approval to recognize people daily. You don't need budget to ask how people are feeling.

Start with what you control. Your team. Your fifteen minutes. Your consistency.

Do it for 30 days. Track the results. Then bring the story up.

Step 2: Build the Business Case

Executives don't care about feel-good culture initiatives. They care about metrics that impact the bottom line.

Speak their language.

"Our voluntary turnover costs us $X annually. If we reduce turnover by 25% using a system that costs $Y, the ROI is Z. Here's proof from our pilot."

Use the data from Chapter 2. Turnover costs $3,500-$7,500 per hourly employee. Safety incidents cost thousands in workers' comp and lost productivity. Disengaged employees cost 18% of their salary in lost productivity. [8]

Frame this as a cost-reduction strategy, not a culture experiment.

Step 3: Address the Objections Proactively

Don't wait for "we don't have time" or "this is flavor-of-the-month." Acknowledge those concerns upfront and explain how this is different.

Use the language from Chapter 11. Show you've thought through the objections and have answers.

The Truth About Starting

There will never be a perfect time.

You'll always be busy. There will always be a crisis. There will always be a reason to wait. But waiting is a decision. And that decision has a cost.

Every day you don't start is another day of turnover you could have prevented, engagement you could have built, and performance you could have unlocked.

The Performance Habit works because it's daily. The compound effect works because it compounds. You can't compound what you don't start.

So start.

Chapter 13 References:

[8] Gallup. *"How to Improve Employee Engagement in the Workplace."*
https://www.gallup.com/workplace/285674/improve-employee-engagement-workplace.aspx

Appendix: ROI Calculator

U se this calculator to estimate the financial return of implementing the Performance Habit system.

Step 1: Calculate Your Turnover Cost

Current Annual Voluntary Turnover:

Number of employees: _____

Current turnover rate: _____ %

Number of employees lost annually: __ (employees × turnover rate)

Cost per replacement:

Conservative estimate: $5,000 per hourly employee

(Includes recruiting, onboarding, training, lost productivity)

Use higher estimate for skilled positions: $7,500-$15,000

Annual turnover cost: ___ (employees lost × cost per replacement)

Example:

- 100 employees at 80% turnover = 80 replacements/year
- 80 replacements × $5,000 = $400,000 annual turnover cost

Step 2: Estimate Turnover Reduction

Based on case studies, organizations implementing the Performance Habit system reduce turnover by 30-50% within 12-18 months.

Conservative estimate: 30% reduction

Moderate estimate: 40% reduction

Aggressive estimate: 50% reduction

Projected annual savings:

Current turnover cost: _____

× Reduction percentage: _____ %

= Annual savings: _____

Example (30% reduction):

- $400,000 × 30% = $120,000 annual savings

Notes and Citations

All references used throughout this book are compiled here for easy access.

[1] BizLibrary. "Learning Retention: The Key to Employee Training." https://www.bizlibrary.com/blog/learning-methods/learning-retention-key-employee-training/

[2] Knowledge Anywhere. "Seventy Percent of Your Training is Forgotten: Learn the Science of Knowledge Retention." https://knowledgeanywhere.com/articles/seventy-percent-of-your-training-is-forgotten-learn-the-science-of-knowledge-retention-and-how-it-affects-online-training/

[3] WayWeDo. "The Forgetting Curve: Why Documentation and Training Fails." https://www.waywedo.com/blog/forgetting-curve/

[4] Tallyfy. "Why Documentation Training Fails: The Forgetting Curve." https://tallyfy.com/products/pro/tutorials/why-documentation-training-fails-forgetting-curve/

[5] eLearning Industry. "Employee Training Statistics, Trends and Data." https://elearningindustry.com/employee-training-statistics-trends-and-data

[6] Ferris State University. "How to Retain 90% of Everything You Learn." https://www.ferris.edu/university-college/firstgen/student-handbook/howtoretain90.pdf

[7] BetterUp. "The Value of Belonging at Work: Investing in Workplace Inclusion." https://www.betterup.com/blog/the-value-of-belonging-at-work

[8] Gallup. "How to Improve Employee Engagement in the Workplace." https://www.gallup.com/workplace/285674/improve-employee-engagement-workplace.aspx

[9] Gallup. "State of the American Manager: Analytics and Advice for Leaders." https://www.gallup.com/workplace/231593/state-american-manager-report.aspx

[10] People Management. "'Accidental managers' without proper leadership training contributing to almost one in three workers walking out, research finds." https://www.peoplemanagement.co.uk/article/1844443/acciden tal-managers-without-proper-leadership-training-contributing-almost-one-three-workers-walking-out-research-finds

[11] Fortune. "More than two-thirds of bosses are 'accidental managers'—and their requests for proper training are being ignored." https://fortune.com/2024/05/23/accidental-managers-no-training-losing-talent-survey/

[12] Forbes. "New Research Unlocks the Secret of Employee Recognition." https://www.forbes.com/sites/joshbersin/2012/06/13/new-research-unlocks-the-secret-of-employee-recognition/

[13] Gallup. "State of the Global Workplace Report." https://www.gallup.com/workplace/349484/state-of-the-global-workplace.aspx

About The Author

Dr. Sharon Grossman is the founder of Turnkey Retention Solutions and a leading expert in transforming organizational culture through systematic daily practices.

With over two decades of experience as a psychologist and in leadership development, Sharon has worked with companies across industries to reduce turnover, improve engagement, and build sustainable high-performance cultures.

Dr. Sharon's approach is rooted in a simple truth: culture isn't built through annual events or motivational speeches. It's built through small, consistent deposits made every single day. The Performance Habit methodology grew from this insight and has been implemented in hundreds of operations, producing measurable improvements in retention, safety, quality, and employee satisfaction.

Before founding Turnkey Retention Solutions, Sharon worked with executives to help them recover from burnout through her program, Exhausted to Extraordinary. Her work has been featured in Business Insider, USA Today, and Katie Couric Media, and she is a sought-after speaker on topics including retention strategy, frontline leadership development, and burnout.

Dr. Sharon lives in Miami Beach with her husband and two kids. When she's not helping organizations build better cultures, she enjoys performing improv comedy and traveling the world.

Connect with Dr. Sharon

Website: www.TurnkeyRetention.com

Email: sharon@turnkeyretention.com

LinkedIn: linkedin.com/in/sharongrossman

Acknowledgments

This book exists because of the leaders who were willing to try something different.

To the frontline supervisors who showed up every morning at 6:45 AM to do their first Daily Dialogue, even when it felt awkward and forced—thank you. You proved that consistency beats perfection.

To the executives who took a risk on a pilot program when "we don't have time" was the prevailing sentiment—thank you. Your willingness to test the system made scaling possible.

To Jorge Torres, whose original Performance Habit methodology provided the foundation for this work. Your insights into inputs versus outputs and the power of repetition changed how I think about culture change.

To the employees who scanned the barometer honestly, raised improvement opportunities, and recognized their peers—thank you. You made the system work because you engaged with it authentically.

To the clients who let me learn alongside you as we implemented this system in real-world conditions with real constraints—your feedback, pushback, and partnership made this methodology stronger.

And finally, to every person who's ever felt invisible at work—this book is for you. You deserved better. Hopefully, this gives your leaders a roadmap to do better.

The Performance Habit isn't complicated. But it matters.

Thank you to everyone who helped prove that.

Other Books By Dr. Sharon

The Burnout Solution: 7 Steps from Exhausted to Extraordinary

Motivated to Stay: 100 Strategies for Keeping Your Best People

The Stress Advantage: Lessons from the Tennis Court

Wheely Good Team Building: A Roller Skating Retreat to Revive a Company

The Currents of Change: How to Thrive During Corporate Transitions

The Zen of Work: Transforming the Tension in Your Brain, Body, and Business

Connect With
Dr. Sharon Grossman

To discuss what's going on in your organization, why people are leaving, and how I can help, schedule a 15-minute discovery call: drsharongrossman.com/discovery

If you'd like to bring me in to speak at your next conference on employee retention or burnout, let's talk: https://drsharongrossman.com/bookme

Speaking Testimonials

Sharon is one of the great speakers I heard about beating burnout.

Blenda Larioza, Registered Nurse Alberta Health Services

I always knew what my mindset was capable of, but Sharon's session taught me how to access my capability in a more in-depth manner from a new direction of thinking.

Debra Mcdougall, Psychologist University of Calgary

Extremely motivational! We all get stuck and this allowed us to take a step back and recognize it and take action moving forward!

Carianne Giersch, Customer Success Manager Athena Health

Sharon's presentation was engaging and full of tools to help people deal with anxiety, stress and burnout. I would highly recommend Sharon as a speaker at conferences and to all levels and areas of your organizations.

Alan Vanderburg, Consultant Manager Tulsa County

www.ingramcontent.com/pod-product-compliance
Lightning Source LLC
Chambersburg PA
CBHW071204200326
41519CB00018B/5359